LIVE CAMP WORK

How to Make Money
While Living in an RV & Travel Full-Time.

Sharee Collier

BOOK REVIEWS

"Live Work Camp is a great resource for those looking to explore ways to make money on the road. Having access to a wide range of resources from workcamping all the way to fully remote careers in so many different forms (blog, courses & podcast) is invaluable!"

-Melanie Carr, Vice President of Escapees RV Club
www.Escapees.com & www.RVerJobExchange.com

"There's a ton of information about workamping on the internet today, but few resources provide such detailed tips about how to get started the right way and what to expect once you're employed."

-Rene Agredano, Full-time RVer
www.LiveWorkDream.com

This book is packed with great information and links to prospective job leads. I read it in one day and was very impressed. We have been full-timers for 3 years now and we have never had a problem establishing a workamping position.

She covers tons of great items and the booked is packed with fantastic helpful information. I especially liked the info on how to use volunteer.gov and bid with Corps of Engs. as we have always worked in private campgrounds. I would say this book needs to be a regular in any RVers library if you are considering workamping. Well written and very informative!

-Susan Anderson

As a full-timer who has worked some of the jobs Sharee covers, I can attest to the accuracy and value of the information she shares in her book. I wish it was available 4 years ago when I started workamping lol! Sharee lets you know up front what is not covered in her book so your expectations will be on par with what she does share.

This book provides the guidance curious folks need to get started in workamping and tons of additional resources that are even helpful to seasoned workampers. The materials Sharee shares via her VIP mailing list are perfect companions for this book, too. Nothing she does is redundant. She has mapped out a flexible plan with the checklists you need, too. I highly recommend this book to anyone considering the RVing work camping lifestyle!

-Adrienne D. Cruser

This book was a quick read and had some good information on how to find work on the road, while camping, or full-time RVing. As a full-time RVer, we have had some of these work experiences and it was fun to read about others experiences and ideas. I have done lots of research, read many articles, blogs, etc on workamping and this one had some of the most original ideas I have seen so far. If you are new to workamping or a seasoned RVer, this will appeal to you.

-April Renee

My husband and I are looking into the work kamping lifestyle and had no idea where to start or if this was even a possibility or just a dream. This has so many helpful tips about the lifestyle, jobs, pay and reality of work kamping. I recommend this book to anyone who is looking to get away from the stressful day to day lifestyle and try something new and exciting. My husband and I now know what to expect and how start traveling for a living! Thank you Sharee for putting together such an informative book!

-Monica Thompson

This is an awesome book to read! Very informative and easy reading. I am so excited to start my life as a full-time RVer soon and this book has some very needed information. Thank you so much Sharee for this!!

- Lisa Stewart

Live Camp Work
Print Edition
Sharee Collier

ISBN-13: 978-0-578-46391-9

Legal Disclaimer:

Please note that most of the information contained within this publication is based on personal experience. Although the author and publisher have made every reasonable attempt to achieve complete accuracy of the provided content, they assume no responsibility for errors or omissions of any kind. Any and all trademarks, service marks, product names or named features are assumed to be the property of their respective owners and are used only for reference. There is no implied endorsement, to any degree.

This book is dedicated to my loving family.

Without you there would be no family adventure or wild travel tales of a life spent living on the road free to roam. Thank you for always supporting my crazy ideas! Especially the one when I said, *"Let's live in an RV!"*

Without you this book would not be possible!

I love you to the moon and back-

SPECIAL THANKS

I need to give a special thanks to everyone in my life who has supported my wild ideas especially the dedicated group of fellow working RVers who graciously helped me bring the final product to market.

I asked for your comments, thoughts and suggestions and you willingly supplied me with genuine insights, thoughtful commentary, and helpful guidance.

You helped me sculpt the final book into a resource that has helped thousands decide if working on the road while in an RV is right for them!

This kind of support is only available from inside the RV community, of which I am so proud to have been a part of for so many great years!

Thank you all so much.

I am forever grateful!

TABLE OF CONTENTS

INTRODUCTION

Hey there! I'm Sharee Collier.

My husband Antwon and I have been traveling for the past 6 years with our 4 great kids trying to see and do as much as possible on a super road trip we started back in 2013!

Non-traditional life for us started a few years before that! Back in 2010 to be exact. Back then we were pretty normal and basically did what everybody else did.

- We lived in a house with a two-car garage.
- We worked 9-5 jobs.
- Our kids were in a traditional school.
- We had 2 cars and a dog...

As you can imagine, that normal (aka boring) list goes on and on.

SOMETHING DIFFERENT

But one day, we woke up! We woke up with the idea to stop. Stop trying to fit in. Stop trying to get 1st place in the rat race. Stop living inside the box. We woke up and wanted nothing more than to just get out and explore. So, we made a short list of 3 possible adventures...

"Live at the beach.
Live in an RV.
Live on a sailboat."

We started with #1 of course!

We loved it. The kids loved it. We could walk through the sand dunes and into the water in 2 minutes flat, and then be back home for lunch or dinner just as quick.

This was fun for a while, but then one day, the kids were literally swimming with sharks. Then another day my husband almost got washed into the water (with the car) as the first day of hurricane season arrived. Then one day, shortly after, we decided we were really landlubbers and being close to the water, was pretty for a short vacation, but not so much our thing… as far as life goals were concerned.

'We started with a simple google search.'

Researching camping, extended road trips, living in an RV, and how to work and travel. It all looked very exciting and like something we thought for sure would make some great memories- so why not give it a try??

RV LIFE BEGINS

Next, we looked for an RV we could afford and paid cash.

After a quick interior rehab, some maintenance to the engine and a new braking system, we moved into our new home on wheels… A 1973 Winnebago Brave. Since our new home was actually older than any of us, we made the decision to baby it for a while with short trips!

Simple right? Well, sort of! I mean it wasn't as difficult as some people make it out to be. But then again, we didn't go through many of the fears other people face, like downsizing, getting rid of possessions, or being crammed into 200sq ft with your spouse, or the whole family in our case.

We attacked our goal of RV life as a positive experiment.

All along we knew if we didn't like it or couldn't make it work, we could always go back to doing what everybody else was. And while not the most comforting of backup plans, it was a safe option we were very comfortable with navigating if need be.

To be completely transparent, RVing full-time may not have worked out for us without the concept of workamping, which is where you work while you RV, you know so you can keep a steady stream of income as you explore (basically- what this whole book is about)!

It's true. Workamping provided a quick and easy ticket for us to travel. And it did so without the need for retirement income, a huge savings account, a remote job or even a location independent small business.

All we had to do was find short-term, seasonal jobs in places we wanted to visit. That was half the battle, and once we had a job- the travel centered around it pretty seamlessly. What made it even better was that some employers offered free or reduced camping!

You can do it if you really want.

Workamping is a simple idea that so many people have a hard time grasping! It leaves so much for the individual to decide upon and design for themselves, that many people get overwhelmed with the possibilities and the freedom to use it as you wish. After spending 6 years workamping in various forms, I think it's time I give a more detailed explanation of the lifestyle for those who are just tuning in!

WHAT'S IN THIS BOOK

In this book, I'd like to help clarify common misconceptions that plague the minds of many people considering whether or not workamping can help them hit the road sooner than retirement, post-retirement, or when retirement isn't even in sight! By providing necessary information about the Live Camp Work community and the variety of available employment opportunities.

If you'll keep an open mind and a positive outlook, I'll walk you through the basics, dive into the types of jobs available with specific employers, and even provide over 1,000 employers who hire RVers, as well as seasonal workers to get you started faster than you ever dreamed.

"Live Camp Work will help you get started, go farther, or keep going."

SECTION 1

WORKAMPING BASICS

If you haven't heard by now, workamping is the adventurous life of work and RV travel! It has grown in popularity over the past decade and stories of its alternative lifestyle have made news headlines from the Seattle Times to the Huffington Post and even a segment on NBC's Today Show!

Media and news reports say people are turning to alternative ways of living and RVing is at the top of the list. More people are currently living in RVs in the US than ever before and while most people hear the word workamping (or work camping) and immediately think of retirees, it's not always the case. People who work while they RV come from a variety of backgrounds, ethnicities and age demographics and have all taken kindly to the RVing lifestyle for the vast benefits it affords them.

With such a broad definition there is bound to be some confusion and general questions that everyone will want to know the answers to. In this section, I'll walk you through workamping basics discussing what exactly all this means.

WHAT IS WORKAMPING

When I mention the word workamping in a group of people, usually at a campground or RV park, there is always someone in the group who looks confused by what I'm talking about. Either they're new to RVing or just haven't come across the term yet in their travels. In the same group, there is also always someone ready to help explain the details about how workamping is really just for retirees, which is just not accurate.

To make it simple, I usually interrupt and start from the top. While I could easily stay quiet and keep all the good jobs for myself, I figure the more folks I talk to, the faster the word will spread and the bigger the Live Camp Work community will grow. So, I might as well start from the top!

It all started with retirees and camp hosting positions, but as we all know... things change.

AN EVOLUTION IN PROCESS

A small group of retired professionals taking short-term positions as they travelled across the country were coined as "working campers" about 30 years ago. The word was then trademarked and monetized into a paid membership of camp host jobs through newsletters and access to employers. The lifestyle of working as you travel would continue to develop and attract the attention of seniors across the map for years down the road.

For many years the world of working RVers would continue to grow and develop as more and more people took their retirement on the road and worked as camp hosts at various state parks, national parks and forests, as well as private campgrounds across the US.

"Naturally, workamping has evolved to fit the needs and wants of the RV community

over the past 30 years."

What was once mostly retirees taking their funds on the road for adventures at the best national parks throughout the land, has now turned into one of the fastest growing alternative lifestyles the US has ever seen. Workamping now includes a growing population of younger campers from ages 18 – 55. Many have no desire of the traditional life of 9-5 jobs, spending countless hours commuting to and from work, doing yard work on the weekends and quietly reading about amazing places in great books by the fireplace. These folks want to see and do as they please.

Many just want to blow into a new destination, conquer all it has to offer, then blow out again like a cool summer breeze. These are the folks who are shaking up the traditional and bringing workamping into the future.

They bring fresh ideas, life experience, new energy and mounds of great ideas employers are eager to utilize! If this sound like you, you're probably perfect for workamping!

RV + WORK = TRAVEL

With all of this in mind, you might still be wondering, "What is workamping?"

and for you my inquisitive friend, I'd like to offer a simple answer… anything you want!

Workamping can literally be anything you want it to be. For my family, we started with a dream of exploring the United States. Goals of taking our kids on an endless adventure where small and big discoveries would roll seamlessly into everyday life and family memories would easily be attained through cherished moments together as perpetual travelers. We fell into workamping after a few internet searches of 'working + RVing' and came across a program called Camperforce by Amazon.

Working for Camperforce is probably the farthest you can get from the traditional RV life and expectations of workamping, which for us seemed perfect for young folks just starting out. But like many others we would soon figure out that this gig is hard work and takes more than just the ability to stand for extended periods of time to make it through and still keep your smile! (We'll talk more about this later.)

So back to my original point, if you live in an RV, regardless of if you are full-time, part-time or seasonal, and you're working seasonal jobs, then you're probably workamping. Let's look at some basic examples

WORKAMPING EXAMPLES

- Volunteering as a Docent
- Camp Hosting at a State Park
- Selling Campground Maps & Advertising
- Operating a Small Business
- Selling Crafts at Fairs & Festivals
- Working as an RV Technician or Mobile Repair Service
- Being a Wagon Master for RV Caravans
- Providing Security at an Oil Field Gate

Since workamping can be so inclusive, it's best to be broken down into smaller categories that make it easier to follow.

I like to think of it in terms of Seasonal Jobs (the largest), Location Independent Jobs, Small Businesses & Traditional Jobs.

SEASONAL JOBS

The majority of workamping job opportunities fit into the category of seasonal jobs. They benefit both the employer and the RVers from this perspective.

Employers are looking for the perfect hires! They need a specific number of reliable employees to come help them out in their busy seasons and then leave when the season is over.

RVers, on the other hand, want to stay in the best locations during the high season and leave when the weather turns to the undesirable type and make some cash to cover expenses.

The intersection where the needs and wants of both sides meet is the picture-perfect place where happy RVers & employers thrive.

WHY CHOOSE A SEASONAL RV JOB?

Choosing to work in locations during what is considered the workamping season, or any season for that matter, is a decision to stay put for a specific amount of time.

For some, the thought of traveling to a job with the requirement of living in the location for 3-6 months is madness. For others, who see the benefits of traveling slow and working along the way, it brings a variety of adventures season after season.

Since seasonal jobs are the most widely advertised positions, they are also the easiest type of workamping job to find and acquire. Job sites across the web are filled with advertisements asking RVers to fill a variety of positions ranging from Site

Hosts to Ranch Hands and from Front Desk & Reservations to Grounds, Maintenance & Housekeeping.

WHAT KINDS OF JOBS ARE AVAILABLE?

In a seasonal role, you will have the ability to stay in awesome locations and destinations some people can only dream about spending more than a few days!

These locations can include State & National Parks, like Yellowstone or Glacier. It could also mean working more physical positions like Amazon Camperforce and/or the Sugar Beet Harvest to meet your savings goals, possibly without much need for other gigs.

Positions range from one end of the spectrum to the other and include everything from those mentioned above to food service, housekeeping, working at shooting ranges, activity planning, membership sales, events, festivals and much more.

Most of the positions advertised can be done by just about anyone with a can-do attitude, a willingness to help in more than one area, and a flexible schedule.

To be successful and find jobs easily, you will need a new outlook on what jobs you find attractive. In exchange for a life of travel that allows you to go now rather than later, you will need to figure out what you are willing to do and what you are not.

"Many workamping jobs do not require vast amounts of previous experience, additional certifications, or extensive skills"

•

34 IDEAS FOR SEASONAL WORKAMPING JOBS

1. Gate Guarding
2. On-Site Security Personnel
3. Tour Guide
4. Ski Resort Staff
5. Harvest Employee
6. Volunteer in State Parks
7. National Park General Staff
8. Historical Docent
9. Off- Season Property Caregiver
10. Christmas Tree Lot Managers
11. Pumpkin Lot Managers
12. Firework Sales
13. Dog Show Judge
14. Amusement Park Staff
15. Casino Staff
16. Bus/Shuttle Driver
17. Sporting Event Staff
18. Playing Santa Claus
19. RV Caravan Wagon Master
20. RV Deliveries
21. Visitor Center Worker
22. Maintenance
23. Mystery Shopper
24. Circus Workers
25. RV Inspectors
26. NASCAR Circuit Workers
27. Horse Wrangler
28. Backcountry Patrol
29. Park or Gate Attendant
30. Census Taker
31. Tax Preparer
32. Warehouse Worker
33. Festival Booth Setup
34. Craftsperson

LOCATION INDEPENDENT

A new catchy phrase for a job category we've seen spike in recent years, thanks to the digital era and the love of mobile technology, are location independent jobs.

Having Location Independence means that you can work from anywhere! Location independence is the ability to not have to stay in one location for any specific amount of time or for any specific reason.

As you can imagine, this is a very attractive job category!

Many people who dream of a life full of travel, actually have their sights set on location independence, where they wander freely from place to place, working whenever and wherever they see fit.

I'll admit, the life of a location independent nomad with no ties to geography or agreements to work in one location for set amounts of time, with freedom to explore the surrounding areas at a whim, is pretty awesome. But it does seem less attainable for the majority of people.

These positions can vary from a range of tech support careers to customer service representatives and even direct sales positions. They may not be for everyone, but they offer benefits that are very attractive to RVers wishing for a free style of travel with added flexibility.

SMALL BUSINESSES

One of the best ways to hit the road with little to no strings attached is to own and operate your very own small business from the comfort of your RV.

Small business owners across the country are finding that RV life affords them the comforts of home, a stable office environment and the freedom to roll wherever the road leads! Running a small business is hard work but can be a very rewarding career strategy for those who have the entrepreneurial spirit and the drive to make it all happen.

Since running a small business from your RV can include just about any business, or hobby for that matter, as long as you are able to generate a steady income stream, the options are limitless.

Some folks start with a hobby they love and turn it into a revenue stream after investing some time and energy to build a client/customer list that can sustain them as they travel. Others find it easier to start a small business and build it around the direct sales or affiliate marketing concepts.

However, you find is the best way to build a business you can run from the road, I would recommend you do so.

I love the idea of having multiple income streams! And while your business may not be able to fully fund your travel and cover all your expenses from the start, it can add extra cash to the pot. As it grows, the revenue, freedom to set and exceed your own goals, make the big decisions, and the ability to do what you love on your terms, are all benefits unmatched by any employer.

TRADITIONAL JOBS

When I speak of traditional jobs, I'm referring to jobs for companies that do not offer a campsite or make any reference in their hiring or recruiting strategies to hiring RV workers in particular.

These companies generally are just looking to hire from the local employment pool and have no interest in how or where you might reside. They either stumble across the working RV employment niche and decide hiring a mobile workforce is a great new idea or you find them. In either case, the reasons for and benefits of working such a job can only be measured on a case-by-case basis.

Traditional jobs can include retail positions, tech companies, customer service, call centers, maintenance jobs and anything else you can dream of.

To be honest, the only way they even fit into the conversation of workamping is that you are living in an RV while you work.

Now that you have an understanding of what workamping is and what types of workamping jobs are available, let's go on to Chapter 2 where we will make sure to dig into the top four questions pertaining to living in an RV and working while you travel!

WORKAMPING QUESTIONS

There are many questions pertaining to the lifestyle of living, camping and working in your RV, but in this chapter, I'm going to tackle the top four:

- why people start workamping
- where you can go
- what you can do and
- how much you can make

my main goal is to provide you with vital information from the start. After all, it's usually helpful to know the backstory before you dive headfirst into something!

Q. WHY DO PEOPLE START WORKAMPING?

The number one reason people decide to go workamping is freedom.

Freedom of location that is.

Very similar to location independence, having freedom of location allows for RVers to make seasonal moves, with some control over the timing and length of stays in each destination.

Freedom of location is basically the ability to not be fully confined by a specific geographic area for one reason or another. It allows ordinary people, like you and me, to explore and create adventures that we wouldn't typically be able to have if we worked a regular 9-5 job and stayed in one place all year long.

"Workamping gives people from all walks of life, all backgrounds and all ethnicities the ability to travel."

With the nomadic roots of the workamping jobs, you are instantly able to go wherever you want, do whatever you want and stay as long as you want as long, as you can find an employment opportunity.

Doesn't that sound awesome?

DITCHING THE NORM

When my family first set out to RV in 2013, this was advantage number one on our list!

We wanted to explore! We wanted to see the other 49 states and we wanted to be able to do it with four kids in tow - while making money along the way. Workamping allowed us to check all those boxes and thus we pegged it as our ticket to travel!

For six years, it has led us down some pretty amazing roads and to and from some awesome adventures. Without the ability to work in various locations, which ultimately led me to create the Live Camp Work community, we would still be living the *standard American life,* without knowing if that's truly what we wanted.

Being working RVers gave us the option to choose for ourselves and decide as we saw fit.

Many people I've met along our journey have had similar tales- they wanted to do something adventurous for a while, usually saying they would RV for 1 year as a break. They wanted to exit the rat race and live a little.

Some decided to put those lifelong careers on hold for a year and explore. Others knew from the start they never wanted to return to their sticks and bricks (traditional housing) but they were apprehensive about how it would all work out in the end.

The idea to Live Camp Work gave them a chance to ditch it all and just start something fresh! Something full of adventures. Working while they RV, gives them the ability to do it now rather than later.

It can do the same for you.

They liked the workamping lifestyle because it allowed them to start sooner than the typical retirement age and they could do it for as long or as short of a time span as they wished. Workamping may have evolved over the last 30 years, but the benefits remain the same!

THE PERKS

We've met people who have worked along the way for 20+ years and have no desire to stop any time soon. They have incredible adventures, and many will tell you amazing stories about being able to live in places like Yellowstone National Park for six months out of the year!

That's insane…

Do you know how much it would cost to rent a campsite in Yellowstone for six months?

We're talking thousands of dollars! But these people didn't have to pay that type of money for their sites. They were workamping for the National Park Service and their campsites were heavily discounted to about $30 a week plus they were being paid for all hours worked! You can't beat it!

"Can you imagine being a snowbird at the age of 24? 37? 48?"

Even 55 was a bit of a stretch before the idea to Live Camp Work was so widely accepted in the past several years! But now the door is open for everyone. Access to information and jobs has been made easy and free! You no longer have to be part of specific clubs, memberships or organizations- all you really have to do is know where to look to find what you need.

That means, for me at least, I can enjoy my ideal temperature range all year long! Cool summers, warm winters and tons of tourist attractions to keep us all busy are just a few of the reasons why people choose to work while they RV.

Q. WHERE CAN I GO?

This is an easy one… you can go anywhere in the U.S. and work while you travel. You can also go to Canada and Mexico if you are so inclined, but you likely won't be working in those locations.

Maybe start in the east and drive out to the wild wild west. How about starting in the north and then driving all the way down I-95 to Key West for the winter? There's no right or wrong way to travel and you can define your route as you see fit!

The real question is, where you want to go? Or maybe, where have you never been?

Asking yourself one of these questions should get the gears moving!

AN EASY OPTION

Perhaps the easiest way to figure out where you want to go is by starting with your favorite part of the country.

Think about places you've taken trips to and really wanted to stay for more time. Think about those hot tourist destinations you've read about in travel magazines at the grocery store and always dreamed of going. Think about family and friends you wished you could visit and spend more time with on birthdays and holidays!

These are the places you should be going as you Live Camp Work!

Figure this out and you've just started the very first step in planning your adventure! You'll also be one step closer to getting on the road and making money while you travel.

Workamping can provide you with a modest reliable income. It can also provide decreased expenses allowing for you to make special trips to places you've always dreamed of going.

This is exactly how working RVers should plan their trips... with special adventures in mind.

While you can only accomplish a very limited amount of local sightseeing, activities, and attraction visits in any vacation or holiday trip, you will now have the ability to stay in locations for extended periods allowing for more in-depth coverage of each destination if you wish.

Enjoy more time to explore popular destinations and more time to experience the local scene in a destination you always dreamed about. This is how working RVers experience the country one job at a time.

As a working RVer you can go wherever the road leads. The world is wide and the adventures are long, plan your journey for one season, one year or many more.

Q. WHAT CAN I DO?

The real question is what can't you do? And the answer is nothing!

Working RVers have the freedom to choose jobs for short periods, whole seasons, or for longer if they want. They also choose the type of work they want to commit to for each particular job arrangement.

You can try popular positions like reservations and housekeeping or venture into more specific roles like activity and recreation planning, order fulfillment, harvest worker, and many others.

If you find the current position doesn't suit your skills, your needs or your wants for this moment in your life, then just line up something different for future positions and keep going.

The most enjoyable times working come into play when you are able to find jobs doing things you will enjoy and are at the very least comfortable with. It also happens when you are in a destination you enjoy and find interesting, as you will want to make plans during your free time to get out and explore locally.

> *"I can confirm, that the majority of businesses currently advertising for RV positions are campgrounds and RV parks."*

But to be honest, I think this is just because it is where the niche originated, and these employers are more familiar with the term.

We have seen a tremendous outreach from mainstream employers like Amazon, trying to find ways to incorporate their own seasonal workforce of RVers. I believe the need for such a reliable and well diverse employment pool is highly sought after.

As more employers find ways to incorporate this community into their hiring and recruitment initiatives, we will continue to see the offerings for more mainstream or traditional jobs being advertised.

OUTSIDE THE BOX

(Q) Will you find other employers who are hiring RVers? Yes.

Q) Will you find employers who are looking for people to stay onsite? Yes.

Q) Will you find employers who offer onsite housing options such as cabins or mobile homes? Yes.

And while all these job opportunities are essentially workamping, they just have not yet accepted the term and as a result, miss the mark when trying to recruit.

Don't let that discourage you!

Workamping jobs and opportunities are all around us - all you have to do is dig them out! Look for employers advertising keywords in their ads and on the employment pages of their websites.

If you're looking for a position at a ranch, search the page for the word 'ranch' and see what comes up. (On most computers this can be done by holding down the 'Control/Command' button and the 'F' key and then typing the word into the search field that pops up.)

Also, it never hurts to think outside the box and reach out to a possible employer to inquire about the opportunity for setting something similar up with their business. You might snag a job for yourself and open their eyes to a whole new world of seasonal employees for future hires!

I know thinking outside the box is easier said than done for some people, but for those who are able to accept a less than traditional definition and refuse to put up defining walls or restrictions, they will be able to grasp the full spectrum of workamping opportunities by keeping the options open.

Think about positions at retail stores (Walgreens and Rite-Aid seem to always be hiring), fulfillment centers like Amazon and JC Penney's, harvest fields (apples, beets, or other crops), festivals, amusement parks, water parks, shooting ranges and more! All of these opportunities are open to those who have an adventurous spirit, a great attitude and the freedom to travel! Keep your mind open to all the possibilities that workamping can open for you, and you'll do just fine!

Q. HOW MUCH CAN I MAKE?

I need to be as upfront as possible with you about the income you can expect from workamping jobs. To be frank, it's not the best and it's definitely not the highest wages you'll likely have made in your life. But it is a modest reliable income that can help get you on the road faster than you thought possible.

A combination of paid positions, non-paid and volunteer positions as well as those that offer a combination, are what you will typically find from RV employers.

Many positions are noted for paying minimum wage or something slightly higher. In some places that means $7.25 an hour, while other places like Washington state you'll get $13.50!

These positions are the most common and include jobs that are easy to acquire and most anyone is capable of completing. They include things like reservations and guest check-ins, housekeeping, landscaping, grounds crew, light maintenance, cash register operations, and activities. For these positions, you can expect to be paid close to the state minimum wage and should use your negotiation power when interviewing to assure you receive the best compensation plan.

> ## "While I love to negotiate, it just doesn't work in every situation."

WORD TO THE WISE:

I'll give you a heads up from one camper to another... negotiating with larger employers with well-established programs that typically hire hundreds of RVers is a waste of time.

Programs like the Sugar Beet Harvest, Camperforce, and even when working for larger camping companies like Equity Lifestyle Services - will limit your ability to negotiate.

Instead of seeing it as a negative, look for the positives like corporate structure, knowledgeable key staff members and the benefits offered.

UNDERSTANDING THE LIFESTYLE

As more and more people take to the streets and decide that traveling in an RV is what they truly desire to do, more and more people lack the basic understanding of the workamping.

Workamping has grown tremendously in popularity and with that growth has come a new set of misconceptions, biases and new ideas as a whole. For instance, the idea that you have to be retired and living well off of savings income or monthly retirement checks has been proven false as more millennials and working age RVers transition into the lifestyle.

Other concerns about realistic living expenses, working for your site and being overqualified for basic jobs give new RVers unnecessary worries before starting their big adventures!

The Live Camp Work community can be a fun and exciting part of your life! I know when we first started, we were filled with the joy of location freedom and the dreams of finding nooks and crannies across the map to explore with our kids.

Working along the way, allowed us to pack up and go as we pleased. It allowed us to discover America on our own terms while making some income to pay our way. It can and will do the same for you if you understand first how it all works!

MAKING SENSE OF DOLLARS

Live Camp Work is a niche lifestyle.

It's an alternative way of living for some and a way to travel for others. For most folks, it is a combination of the all three that seems to allow the best balance.

Workamping can be your ticket to travel when you have limited income from outside sources such as small businesses or hobbies that generate very little. It can allow you to take to the open road pre-retirement and stay afloat, so long as you are willing to make necessary adjustments to how much you pay out in respect to the income you have coming in.

Living in an RV can obviously lower your living expenses and free up cash to do fun things like exploring your new destination, but for some it can also provide the needed slack to pay off debt.

Many people have found this to be true and continue to use it as such.

One thing that has remained the same if not pretty close to constant over the years, has been the cost associated with RVing.

"It's not free living!"

It can be cheaper than a traditional travel lifestyle filled with hotels and even gives the American Dream of owning a home in the suburbs a run for its money, but let's be clear... it's not free living!

Many of the costs associated with RV travel can be greatly reduced and sometimes erased through the decision to work along the way.

Workamping lends its hand to help RVers save cash on things like housing expenses, site rental costs, paying for electricity at monthly sites, and having to pay for use of onsite amenities.

Another huge savings is the fuel, as you will not be driving your RV daily from here to there while workamping.

In fact, workamping will allow you to stay for extended periods of time in some of the most desired locations in the US, where only local driving will be necessary.

2 VIEWS OF WORKAMPING

Overall, workamping was first and remains most commonly known as the optional travel life for adventurous souls who want to spend their days exploring and creating memories while staying active in communities across the US. In this view of the lifestyle, people choose to RV and live happy lives based around exploring new areas.

They enjoy their days in short-term jobs that fuel their adventures and they use their off time to see and do as they please.

On the flip side, some have recently pegged workamping as the fallback plan. A last option for those who fail to attain a standard of success and have no other choice but to wander aimlessly through life or what's left of it in search of low paying jobs as a migrant workforce.

This was obviously not the intent of the workamping lifestyle. The reality is that folks who have hit hardships have found that living in an RV, which offers reduce housing costs, is an attainable option.

While we can't fault onlookers or those who find themselves in such a situation for being resourceful, it does cast a dim light on RVing as a whole. One could also argue the same situation shines a bright light on the issues happening around us that cause the need for cheap housing…

WORKING FOR SITE

A major consideration for people considering workamping is how many hours you will be required to work in exchange for your RV site.

Personally, I like to respond with a big fat ZERO… but sometimes it's just not the case. Some employers will not provide a free campsite as part of your compensation and they will want a set number of hours worked to cover its cost. In this situation, since your job duties will depend on your position and the working environment may or may not be seen as an added benefit along with any other perks, you will need to compute how much you are being asked to pay for your site. Decide if the hours worked are benefitting you, the employer, or both.

Using this formula to compute the value will help you make sure the cost of the site is worth your time and energy:

Monthly Value ÷ Hours = Wage

Monthly Value: is equal to the site rental fee (either based on the monthly or seasonal rate) + monthly utility cost + value of perks or additional benefits provided by employer.

Example:

Step 1: $650 monthly site + $150 utilities + $100 perks = $900 monthly value.

Step 2: $900 monthly value ÷ 80 hours (20 hours required per couple/per week) = $11.25 per hour

In this case, you are being paid $11.25 per hour in exchange for the RV site.

If this ever comes out to even a penny below the minimum wage, I would strongly suggest you rethink the decision to move forward with the job opportunity, unless there are huge benefits to being in that location during the specific time period the job would run.

Also, if there is not a monthly rate available you should use the seasonal rate or something equivalent, but definitely not the daily rate by any means!

It's very typical now to see many jobs offering a site plus pay. These jobs will pay a general range of somewhere between $8.00-$12.00 per hour. If you can confirm a position with an employer who is paying $10.00 or more per hour and offers a FHU (full hook-up) campsite for FREE, you're doing well!

I don't say that to be cute... I say it because it is the absolute truth and I think you need to know this upfront.

I'm trying to set realistic expectations and let you know from the start that you will not get rich workamping! If making big bucks and living lavishly is your thing, this might not be the RV life for you!

Also, now is a good time for me to mention that depending solely on your income from workamping jobs is not a good place to start. Not only have I been there and done it, but I did not enjoy it and it didn't last long.

Workamping is much better lived with some other source of monetary funds flowing in. I like to think of it as a way to decrease costs and help pay the bills. It will not afford you the luxuries of eating out, buying nice things, exploring the top tourist attractions, or even paying off pricey payments for big rigs with big notes.

OVERQUALIFIED? YES INDEED!

Workamping is not a career. You will not easily find career type wages in comfortable desk jobs with employee benefit plans offering a 401K and stock options. But it can still be a fulfilling way to earn some income while you travel!

This lifestyle is typically centered around jobs in the outdoor hospitality industry and you should expect to be offered positions that involve interactions with the public as well as some based on basic computer skills.

It's easy to feel like your past experience in careers that may have dominated your previous life would deem you as overqualified for the majority of workamping positions regularly advertised and you're probably right to feel this way!

"You are likely very over overqualified for 90% of the jobs you will be asked to complete..."

and this makes you the perfect choice for employers!

RV employers are tired of hiring from the local employment pool which includes people too close to home and those who may have just entered the workforce.

They are looking for RVers to diversify their teams! They long for the chance to hire someone with a skill set they can depend on for knowledge as well as the professionalism that comes along with it.

RVers looking to leave behind the pressures of working careers and fast-paced jobs are in luck.

Employers are looking for you! Include details about your field of expertise and areas where you have thrived in the past on your resume. If an employer is looking for someone who has electrical or sales skills, your resume will stand out if you are open to sharing this information!

THINK IT THROUGH

You must think thoroughly about how workamping will fit into your life, or your new life as an RV traveler before you jump in.

Hitting roadblocks are not fun when you don't have the time, patience or available resources to figure your way out. Do yourself a favor and get your house in order before you start this journey. You will be thankful that you did!

KNOWING THE SEASONS

After a long winter, most likely in snowbird destinations like SoCal, the Arizona desert, Central Florida, and Southern Texas, RVers are gearing up all across the country to make their way to their summer positions.

Places like Yellowstone National Park, Camp Gulf RV Park, Adventureland, and a variety of private campgrounds in destinations many tourists can only dream about spending a whole summer, are gearing up to welcome new RV staffers.

"We choose where to go and for how long!"

It's one of the perks of the Live Camp Work lifestyle- *freedom of location!*

Picking up a seasonal gig in that ultra-desirable tourist location and then spending the better part of the travel season getting to really know your surroundings, the community and having a blast exploring locally.

THE WORKAMPING SEASON

What exactly is the workamping Season? Is it the same as the camping season? Do all RV employers hire for the same time frames? These are the questions that many RVers ask time after time!

The official workamping season coincides with the camping season, which starts around Memorial Day and ends right after Labor Day. The exact dates are not defined nor are they important, because not only do employers hire for a variety of start and end dates, they also might ask you to start in the spring or stay through the winter.

During the camping season jobs are plentiful. Employers are also often overwhelmed with the response to their advertising and the interest to their open positions. Competition is higher overall, but can really be competitive for places like Alaska, Seattle, Maine, and National Parks.

Start applying early in the fall/winter and you will be successful in getting a head start on the masses.

Line up your summer gigs before spring starts to make sure you get your perfect position.

The camping season is essentially the easiest time to find work.

The winter, on the other hand, is more of a challenge, so let's spend most of our time in this chapter discussing those details.

THE WINTER SEASON

Family dinners, holiday parties, and for a lot of RVers, the end of the Camperforce season all mark the start of the next leg of their workamping adventure... the winter season.

Workamping during the winter really isn't unusual. It will require a little more planning and forethought than the typical route of securing a job for the camping season, so just plan ahead.

The Winter Season brings a bucket load of questions, tons of uncertainty, and even some restlessness as RVers choose to settle into monthly stays at snowbird-friendly parks in the south and far west, still wondering if they could have found a job for the winter instead.

The idea that working during the winter is minimal - and to some extent none existent - is one to be taken lightly. It's pretty far from the truth if you're willing to step outside your comfort zones, plan ahead, and maybe use some creativity to find a position you feel good about.

FINDING WINTER JOBS

Start with the basics on how you find work for the camping season, add some extra time and keep your eyes open for jobs when they first become available as well as those previously advertised.

"Finding a winter position might be a little easier than you think."

3 RECOMMENDATIONS

Use the information available. Check past and current ads as well as any job alert emails you may have received previously. Sometimes employers will purposely leave out start and end dates in their advertising, to let working RVers know they have positions open during several times of the year.

Take leaps of faith. Sometimes you may have to jump out on a leap of faith by just sending your resume to employers who you may not know for sure are even hiring. The idea here is to get your resume into the hands of the people making the hiring decisions and letting them take it from there. It can't hurt!

Follow-up with each employer. Create a list of the companies you've sent your resume to for follow-up calls. I like to keep an Excel spreadsheet with columns (*employer name, 1st Email, Phone follow-up, 2nd Email, Offer, Confirmed, Notes*). *This method* helps me keep track and remember who I've contacted, who replied, and what the next step is. When you're dealing with multiple employers you need to keep your information organized.

CAN I FIND A JOB NOW?

It's not a straight 'yes' or 'no' answer. There are many people who would swear that they found the perfect job at the very last minute and that their winter worked out great. But there are others whose story is the exact opposite, and you'll likely hear those stories first.

So, I'll just say, there is a chance, but why not just plan ahead and be prepared? Planning ahead is going to be your best tool for success.

RVers, especially those who wish to have the most desirable jobs during the winter, are known for booking jobs 1-3 seasons ahead to make sure they get the job they want the most. Be diligent and get a plan together of the next few seasons. Even a general idea of where you wish to travel will be a big help when you sit down to apply for open positions.

If you can't narrow down the exact location, try to plan what region of the country you'll travel to and look for a job in that area. If you find a great opportunity and are offered a job, base your travels around that location and enjoy what the area has to offer!

The bottom line is, planning ahead will help you plan your adventure and make sure you don't always have to hustle at the end of the summer to find where you'll go next.

AVOIDING POPULAR DESTINATIONS

Florida, Texas, and Arizona definitely attract an insane amount of people in the winter, but don't let that scare you off - just think of it as another part of the adventure. And, if you plan ahead, you could be one of those super prepared RVers who found a sweet gig camp hosting at a beachfront RV resort.

I personally love Florida, so I'd never recommend you stay away. It's an awesome state to live, camp, and work! There are so many attractions, historical sites, beautiful coastlines, and tons of campgrounds to keep RVers as busy as they want, or not at all.

During the winter months, while investigating opportunities for RV jobs in warm destinations, you will often see compensation packages that just include the RV site and perks.

There are fewer offers of paying wages for extra hours or wages for all hours worked. This is likely due to the demand for these warmer locations that provide the employers with more bargaining power.

Many snowbird resorts are constantly full and taking an on-site job in one of these resorts can help you get into an area you may otherwise have to wait years to experience.

A FEW TIPS

- Look for year-round private campgrounds and RV parks.
- Check into volunteer positions with state parks, U.S. Army Corps of Engineers projects, government-run operations, or non-profit organizations in states with warmer winter weather.
- Contact Bowlin Travel Centers about positions in their stores and Dairy Queen restaurants in Arizona and New Mexico.
- Research ski resorts who might need seasonal staff and shuttle drivers.
- Consider positions that you can do anywhere! AGS, Southeast Publications, and Good Sam Travel Guide are three examples where you are selling ads and marketing packages all year long!

WHAT ARE SOME OPTIONS?

Winter jobs exist at state parks, historical sites, private campgrounds, franchise parks, snowbird resorts, travel centers, ski resorts, retail stores, restaurants, and more.

These are all great options to get started with but don't limit yourself. You can find winter workamping jobs scattered throughout the southern half of the United States and much of the West Coast.

Options for working during the winter can be endless, especially if you can consider options besides a traditional campground job.

The best part about RVing is you can do just about anything. I know that sounds cliché, but actually really true.

Workamping doesn't have to just include campgrounds. You don't have to clean cabins and bathrooms, make reservations, or work in warehouses. You can do what you want.

> ## "As working RVers, we choose our jobs for one reason or another."

12 IDEAS FOR WINTER WORKAMPING

1. Trade show booth at RV shows
2. House or property sitting
3. Sell something on Etsy, Amazon, or eBay
4. Workamping at Camp Gulf
5. Work with an established company like All Pro Water Flow
6. Sell photography to Shutterstock
7. Become a mobile RV technician and fix your neighbors' rigs
8. Sell some articles or blog posts
9. Start a dog walking service
10. Winter jobs at the Grand Canyon
11. Get involved with a direct sales distributor like Tupperware, Avon, or Young Living,
12. Camp host in California State Parks

WORKAMPING RESUMES

The top items on the recruitment agenda are resumes, photos, and work agreements.

These three items are the topic of many conversations regarding recruiting RVers and dealing with RV employers, so we need to discuss each one and get comfortable with the expectations!

An employer advertises your picture-perfect opportunity, which you are instantly excited about applying for… you then read that they are requiring a resume as well as photos of yourself and your RV.

"What? Is that legal? Why do they need pictures?"

Many questions start to cloud your judgment on if this is actually as great of an opportunity as you originally thought, and you take a step back to think for a moment. But before you write them off, I urge you to learn more about the working RVer's application process, how it differs from traditional hiring, and what is expected vs. required.

Let's start with resumes!

WORKAMPING RESUMES

A workamping resume is the same as a traditional job resume, it's a tool to sell yourself to employers and grab a job you're interested in. As a sales tool it needs to be well written, well-organized, have a clear objective and be an effective way of lining up interviews.

Ideally, it's a single page document that highlights your abilities and quickly details your past work experience. This can easily spread to 2 pages for a couple or family, which is totally fine!

It's your first impressions and your first chance to make a good impression on the employer, so make sure you take full advantage of this opportunity!

With a sea of probably 100K RVers trying to grab the same workamping jobs, this is the critical point where your first impression will either make or break your chances of being hired.

Making sure your resume has the right information, the right format, the right pictures and a cover letter will take some time to get polished, but it makes a huge difference in who will ultimately get the job and who will not.

What Should Be Included?

- Full names of everyone applying for work.
- Contact information (phone and email)
- Headshot of person(s) who are applying for work.
- Picture showing your RV setup
- Short objective statement that is general enough to cover most jobs you will apply for.
- Employment history for past 10 years. (Or the most recent 3-5 jobs you've had that can relate to those you'd be applying for.)
- Highlights on skills relevant to the job you're apply for.
- Include references or a note that they are available on request.

Workamping Resume Tips:

- Keep it short. 1 page per person.
- Include history outside of workamping jobs. (You should also list past experiences in careers that will give you a leg up with employers looking for seasoned workers with specific skills)
- Break up paragraphs with bullets and bold headings
- Be descriptive about the main responsibilities. (Don't discount your skills! List what you do best and trust that the perfect job opportunity will present itself! At the very least you've done your part by putting it out there. The ball is officially in their court)
- Make notes of volunteer and charity work.
- Have someone proofread it.

MY RESUME STORY

When I created my Workamping resume, I didn't have any workamping experience, so I could only include my past work experience, which I thought would be helpful to almost any employer! That included customer service, tons of computer and web skills, retail and sales experience as well as some event planning.

I didn't use a fancy website resume builder or any tools other than Microsoft Word.

As I began to get job offers from employers who were in dire need of some 'new blood', I saw that not only were these offers being quoted at higher dollar amounts than what was being reported by fellow RVers, but some employers were actually creating positions for me based on my experience and trying to bring in a new surge of fresh energy to their businesses!

WHAT IS A COVER LETTER?

A cover letter is an introduction tool that should always be written for each job and precedes your attached resume. It's a sales tool sent to employers to introduce yourself and your skill set as the solution to their hiring needs.

What Should A Cover Letter Include?

- Contact name of who will read your resume.
- Your full name
- Introduction of yourself and mention of the position you're applying for.
- Link between your skills and the experience required for the job
- Push to view attached resume
- Ask for an interview

Cover Letter Tips:

- Short and simple.
- Don't include the text of your resume

- Check your spelling and grammar
- Use bullets and bold headings where appropriate

BIG RESUME MISTAKES

Resumes are a hard task to tackle. So much so that there are many mistakes commonly made that easily sabotage well-meaning RVers looking to snag competitive positions.

Grammatical & Spelling Errors

Even one error on your resume can make potential employers turn the other way! It's just not professional, and although we're all human and can easily make a quick typing error, your resume is one place you can't afford to have one slip through your editing checks.

Have someone, other than your computer's spell check feature, review your resume for errors! The more eyes the better!

Outdated or No Contact Information

Your contact information needs to be listed not only on your Cover Letter but also clearly at the top of your actual resume in case they are separated.

It's best to make sure you have it in both places to make it easiest on the employer to contact you when they want to set up an interview! Not having this important information on your resume makes it appear to the employer that you possibly do not care, don't pay attention to details and that you are unprofessional. Current email and phone numbers should both be listed.

No Past Employment References

You can provide a killer resume, with the best past employment, skills and experience- but without verifiable references that can answer 'YES!' to the question on whether they would rehire you, you can almost guarantee you won't get the job!

Think about your references and what they will say when asked these questions! Contact your references and make sure it's still appropriate to include them on your resume, especially if it's been several years.

RESUME BUILDERS

Many sites like Escapees, Workers on Wheels and WorkampingJobs have workamping resume builders, that you can use for FREE!

Conveniently, they all host a resume system where employers have the ability to search for applicants. As an RV worker, you'll have the option to be listed in multiple search results which populate depending on their search parameters.

Having your resume online certainly can't hurt your chances of finding great jobs in fun place. And since these are FREE tools to use, why not?

Personally, I'd post my resume to all the FREE sites and then search for jobs as usual. It's more of a backup plan than a Plan A but can be just another way of making sure you're getting the word out that you're looking for jobs!

One thing to note is that you do not need a paid resume builder service to be successful in workamping. The free options are just as good!

And although it does take a lot of the leg work out, remember that none of these builders should be your Plan A.

You always have the option to write, edit and send your resume and cover letter through email to workamping jobs you wish to apply for. This is how I always attack my job hunting, and to be honest this is still the best route to take. Not all employers will have the time to spend searching online builders for applicants.

However, If this option is your chosen path, just make sure you include all the relevant information and make sure to follow the submission requirements and directions noted in the employer's advertisements.

SENDING PHOTOS

Many employers will ask for you to include a photo of yourself and your rig along with your resume.

Many RVers are instantly put off by this practice and question if it's merely a method of discrimination for one reason or another.

> *"I both agree and disagree with the validity of sending pictures to employers."*

While I have participated (in my own way) and encouraged the participation of this recruiting practice, it was for one reason and one reason only…

to avoid myself, my family or any fellow RVer arriving at a job site only to be turned away.

With an ancient motorhome and 4 kids in tow, my husband and I never wanted to arrive at a new job with the employer not knowing exactly what they were getting.

In the beginning, I would silently refuse to send photos, but would casually include a link to our blog with an invitation for the employer to get to know us…

After 2 instances where the employer was shocked after arrival that we were so young and had multiple children, I promised myself I would never drive anywhere until I had clearly laid out in an email with a time stamp, that we had 4 kids, this is what we look like, and this is what we camp in.

There is no way I wanted to drive any distance with the lingering fear of denial or rejection. When people ask me about why I think RVers should just send the pictures, this is what I tell them.

Employers are hiring you virtually.

They are not taking the traditional interview route, which would require you to be present for at least one face-to-face interview. In return for not having to travel to their business for an in-person interview, which I was actually asked to do one time, do yourself a favor and send the photos or agree to a virtual interview over Skype or FaceTime!

WORK AGREEMENTS

Once you have sent your resume, aced the interview and accepted the position, make sure your next step is to get everything in writing!

When I say get it in writing, I don't mean a paper trail of email, although in a pinch this would work as well. I'm talking about a well-detailed work agreement that clearly lays out what is expected of you in your agreed upon position, what the hourly wage will be, how many hours, if any, will be required to pay for your site, among other things that are super important.

You should have this document signed and in hand before raising your jacks to drive off!

Work agreements are not contracts, but they do serve as a common agreement between the employer and the RVer on what was actually agreed upon.

Sometimes you are hired months in advance, and even if that's not the case, sometimes people flat out forget all the details. Then it's simply the employer's word against yours and you might not feel comfortable approaching them about the key differences once you've already arrived.

What to Include in Your Workamping Agreement:

- Employment start and end dates
- How much time before and after employment you will be allowed to occupy the site.

- What type of RV site is provided for your use? FHU? W/E (water and electric)?
- Is the RV site included or do you have to pay for it?
- Can you pay in hours worked? If so, how many per week/per person?
- Your position and the duties that it requires. (Don't assume that reservations won't include cleaning toilets… make sure you know ahead of time, what is required in the position you've chosen to accept.)
- Will you be paid hourly? Is there a monthly stipend?
- Will the value of your RV site be reported on your W-2? Will a 1099 be issued?
- Is there a completion bonus?
- What is the overtime policy?
- What are the benefits other than monetary compensation that the employer is offering you? Wi-Fi? Propane? Golf cart? Free amenity usage? Onsite meals?
- Is there an employee discount? Does it apply to visiting family members and friends?
- Special Arrangements? If you've spoken with the employer specifically about a special arrangement like a preset/fixed schedule or dates that you must have off, you will want to make

sure these items are detailed in full on your work agreement as well!

In a perfect world, the employer would openly and graciously offer such an agreement to each and every working RVer they hired, but this world is far from perfect and that just doesn't happen!

Some employers will be beyond prepared and have theirs sent over the moment you complete the interview; others will have you jump through virtual hoops to acquire one. You'll have to be persistent.

You will likely encounter both types of employers, although I hope you have far less of the latter. Make sure you do your due diligence in securing one for each position, and if you are unable-you'll have to decide if it's worth your time and trouble to make the trip without it.

SINGLE & SOLO RV WORKERS

Workamping is the adventurous life of travel enjoyed by many Americans of all ages.

Traveling from place to place, state to state, and job to job may not be a lifestyle made for everyone, but for many it affords the adventurous life they have always dreamed of while providing a modest income to boot.

"RVers travel as couples, singles, and families with their kids in tow,"

Most have the option and luxury of sharing both the responsibilities of each new job and the lifestyle responsibilities of trip planning, driving, and the not-so-glamorous tasks included with setting up their campsite. But not all RVers come in pairs, and for those who don't, there are often additional worries about finding employers who are willing to hire just one.

While these fears are not to be entirely disregarded, they are a little over exaggerated with the usually negative social media posts that dominate the scene.

KNOWING THE DIFFERENCE

Let's first start by clarifying the key difference between a single RV worker and a solo RV worker...

Single refers to a situation where one person is able/willing to work. This person may or may not be traveling with a partner.

Solo is describing someone who is traveling alone.

Many employers, in my experience, will try their best to fill spots with couples based on the simple fact that they can get two workers that only occupy one site.

IT'S JUST BUSINESS

They're trying to lower their costs while being able to utilize the skills and labor force of two individuals per site compared to just one.

What you need to know is that employers are looking for both, those who can fill one spot and those who fill two. Solo & Single RV workers may not be the majority when it comes to folks who travel, but the reality is that many amazing people do it alone and their numbers are growing. Employers will catch on!

There are also many employers who hire just one worker per site. Some employers only have one available position, or maybe they prefer to not have the possibility of personal issues trickling into the workplace and have made the choice to not hire those who live or travel together.

Either way, it works in your favor.

Embrace these jobs and these opportunities and you'll find there is a variety of options for you to choose from.

WHAT TYPES OF JOBS ARE AVAILABLE?

There are a variety of employers and income opportunities available for Solo & Single travelers. A mix of negotiation skills, creativity and patience is almost always a requirement.

Personally, I also think it's just savvy to ask the employer via email, if they are open to filling a spot with one worker vs, two if their ad specifically mentions a couple.

30 Job Ideas For Single Or Solo RVers

1. Rides Operator
2. Lifeguard
3. Activity Director
4. Food Service Staff
5. Store Clerk
6. Campground Host
7. Raft Guide
8. Tour Guide
9. Docent
10. Groundskeeper
11. Security
12. Gas Line Inspector
13. RV Delivery Driver
14. Mystery Shopper
15. RV Inspector
16. Gate Guard/Attendant
17. Warehouse Worker
18. RV Tech
19. RV Detailing
20. Disaster Relief Worker
21. Shuttle Driver
22. Ski Instructor
23. Event/Fair Staff
24. Sporting Event Staff
25. Pet Grooming
26. Pet Walker/Sitter
27. Writer/Blogger
28. Photographer
29. Advertising Sales
30. Campground Map Sale

SINGLE & SOLO RV EMPLOYERS

Many employers hire one worker, some just don't make a point to directly state this in their recruiting ads.

Others obviously love to recruit two strong workers to fill one RV site but welcome single workers with open arms if and when possible. Many employers would be in favor of one strong worker as compared to a couple where one half is seen as a thorn, so do your best to always inquire with employers about the availability for hiring one person.

In addition to many others, the following employers have said they specifically have positions for Single and Solo RVers, so maybe start with one of these.

Various Locations:

- U.S. Army Corps of Engineers
- Texas Advertising - AGS Publishing
- Southeast Publications
- Express Employment Professionals
- Kitchen Craft
- Amazon Camperforce
- Bowlin Travel Centers
- Southern Cross Corp
- KOA: Kampground of America
- Equity Lifestyle Services/Thousand Trails
- RVing Lifestyle Network Ambassadors
- Sky Thunder Fireworks

State Specific Locations

- Xanterra Glacier National Park Lodges
- California Land Management
- Yogi Bear Camp Resort Wisconsin Dells
- Adventureland Amusement Park, Iowa
- Delaware North at Yellowstone
- Black Meadow Landing, California
- Greenlaw's RV & Tenting Park, Maine
- Yellowstone Silver Co., Montana
- Yellow Jacket Campground, Florida
- Lakeside Camp Park, Michigan
- Klink's Resort, Washington
- Vermilion Valley Resort, California
- Trinity Pines, Texas
- Indigo Bluffs RV Resort, Michigan
- The Cabins at Historic Columbine, Colorado
- Country Oaks Campground, New Jersey
- Cherry Hill Park, Maryland
- Black Bear Campground, New York

- Chocorua Camping Village, New Hampshire
- Three Rivers Resort, Colorado
- Mackinaw Mill Creek Camping, Michigan
- Pine River Lodge, Colorado
- Cottonwood Borco Ranch, South Dakota
- West Crooked Lake Resort, Minnesota
- Shenandoah Hills Campground, Virginia
- Spring Creek Campground, Montana
- Forest Recreation Mgmt., South Dakota
- Oli's Trolley, Maine
- Tall Chief RV Campground, Washington
- Jack's Campers, South Dakota
- Wall Drug Store, South Dakota
- Canyon Enterprises, Inc., Colorado
- Blue Bonnet RV Resort, Texas
- Okefenokee Swamp Park, Georgia
- Wilderness Aware Rafting, Colorado
- Rocky Mountain HI RV Park, Montana
- Partridge Hollow Campground, Massachusetts
- Treeland Resorts, Wisconsin
- Stonebridge RV Park, Texas
- Reelfoot National Wildlife Refuge, Tennessee
- Jekyll Island Campground, Georgia
- Sportsman's Supply Campground & Mountain Cabins, Colorado
- Sundance 1 Resorts, Arizona
- Corrington Enterprises, Alaska
- North Rim Country Store, Arizona
- YMCA of the Rockies, Colorado
- The Willamettan's, Oregon
- Olive Branch Campground, Ohio
- Forever Resorts Parry Lodge, Utah
- Guadalupe-Blanco River Authority, Texas
- Taylor Park Trading Post, Colorado
- Detroit Greenfield RV Park, Michigan
- Idaho State Parks
- Glamis North Hot Springs Resort, California
- River View RV Park, Louisiana
- Cedar Pass Lodge, South Dakota

WITH KIDS IN TOW

Back in 2013 when we hit the road with 4 kids in tow to live a life of RV travel, let's just say it was not the norm.

We were one of just a few families traveling full-time in RVs with the intention to work short-term jobs along the way. Workamping families had not been heard of for the most part and we only met two others during the first year.

Something changed between 2015 and 2016, as we approached another season at Amazon Camperforce in Campbellsville, Kentucky. When we arrived, we were met by an unexpected sweet surprise... families were everywhere, and it totally changed the experience for our kids and further normalized our decision to work and travel!

Over the past several years, we've met several families who travel and many others online that wish to travel in the near future.

Most folks have a ton of questions and while some are specific to their life, the following are almost always asked about.

CAN BOTH PARENTS WORK?

Regardless of whether you need childcare for younger children or not, both parents are able to work while traveling.

This can be accomplished in a variety of ways and all revolve around what you find comfortable. For my husband and I, we choose to work opposite shifts, so we could easily work for the same employers.

We would line up employment at various places and ask if one of us could work in the morning and then the other would work at night.

We weren't particular about having the same off days, as we knew this would only be temporary, and to our surprise and enjoyment, it turned out to be a welcome change to those who wanted the same shifts.

"It always worked out for us!"

A FEW THINGS TO NOTE:

A normal schedule included about 20-30 hours per person. We only worked 40 hours (or more) while working for Amazon Camperforce.

We made the most of our hours worked, by only accepting jobs where the site was offered for FREE and not exchanging hours for the rent.

Working opposite shifts gets old quickly. Not having the same off days as your partner in addition to starting your shift when they are ending their shift means you will not see each other very often.

Scheduling our stays at 4 months or less for these job locations made it more manageable.

HOW MUCH WILL I MAKE?

I like to be very upfront and honest about this topic and may have said it before, but you will not get rich workamping. You will make a decent wage and sometimes be provided a FREE site if you snagged a great position. But you will not be adding to your savings account or retirement fund by any means.

If workamping is your only means of income and you have kids in tow, money will be unreasonably tight, and the adventure will be overshadowed by financial woes. Do yourself a favor and find ways to earn extra income through a small business or income-producing hobby, also known as a side hustle.

WHAT IS A SIDE HUSTLE?

A side hustle is an additional income stream you can rely on for X amount of dollars. It's not your day job, a career or even your main workamping gig- it's literally one or more things you've picked up for extra income on the side. In my opinion, everyone needs at least one side hustle, as multiple income streams are always best.

When we were workamping, we also made money through freelance writing, affiliate sales from our blog, and little side jobs we picked up along the way from talking with fellow RVers, friends and family who needed services like content creation, writing, proofreading, website design, and email management among others.

This also helped us not feel 100% dependent on working 40+ hours at every job. We could easily work 20-30 and have great adventures in our downtime!

IS FINDING JOBS HARD?

I can't say it's harder, because I never actually had a hard time. I can't say it's easy because it took a lot of well-crafted emails to get the jobs we wanted along with a great interview.

I can say, workamping with kids is different from those who do it without. So, you have to attack it differently and master how to pitch yourself to be successful.

For instance, when you see a job posted for a campground position you need to react a little quicker than usual. You don't have time to think about every detail.

Give the employer a quick look, decide if it's something doable and then apply. You can do more research later, after your application or resume has been submitted.

In your email to the employer you'll need to craft a very polite and cheerful introduction including how you are excited about the possibility to join the team at a family friendly establishment, some details about the adults looking for work, maybe a recent accomplishment, and then mention you are part of a traveling family with x number of kids.

Let the employer know about your experience and why you'll be a great addition to the team. I usually added a sentence about how we did not need the same days off, but alternating shifts were preferable.

Include pictures of yourself and the family as well as your RV or insert a link to your blog where they are welcome to go 'meet' your family.

Attach your resume with relevant work experience or just the previous positions that would highlight your skills and send it off.

When it comes to families, I find it's better to show a severe over qualification, than to send too little information and hope they will ask the right questions.

CAN KIDS COME TO WORK?

This is such a tricky question and one that I think cannot just be left to common sense and good judgment.

Bringing small kids or even younger teens into the workplace requires many things, but at least three big assumptions need to align perfectly to, which is usually just not the case.

You are assuming they will behave, (according to your standard) and stay content throughout your shift without needing constant supervision or for you to hover over them.

Your employer, if they are okay with this, is assuming your children are well behaved (according to the employer's standards) and that they will not interfere with your work and in some cases may be able to help.

Everyone is assuming that the kids are aware of how to behave in the work environment, understand their role and the expectations set by you and your employer.

My husband and I worked as property managers for a resort and were faced with this issue more than once. We enjoyed a few well-planned days when our kids were able to come to work with us, which allowed for both of us to work at the same time.

This amounted to my husband and I working with one of our twins by our side and our older girls split up with a park ranger to help with small tasks like refilling drink stations and golf cart patrol during school field trips on property. Easy Peasy! In this example, it worked well.

An example of it not working would be taking your kids to work with you when you are required to work on heavy machinery or in food service.

Another might be having your kids hang out with you in the office which is probably not ideal in the eyes of the employer or customers both in person and on the phone.

So, I guess it just really depends on what you're doing, where you're employed, and what the rules of the property are. Keep in mind it could also be doable on one day and then a totally unrealistic request on another.

I advise going into the situation with an open slate. If having the kids come to work with you is the only way to make it work, be upfront and honest with the employer from the beginning.

You never want to travel any distance with the looming possibility that you may be turned away or asked to leave earlier than expected.

ARE EXTRA HOURS REQUIRED?

Occasionally an employer will come up with the new idea that requiring extra hours for people workamping with kids is a perfect solution to keeping things fair. So instead of all sites costing the same amount of trade hours, they'll charge hours based on a per person rate, as in extra hours for each kid.

"This is not a reasonable requirement by the employer."

If hours are being required to cover the cost of the site, which I seriously think you should try to negotiate to be completely FREE, you should not have to work extra hours to cover the kids' stay. It's one RV, on one site. So, it should all be one price.

For example, I once applied to work at a family-friendly property in New York. During the second conversation with the owner of the property, I was told that 10 hours would be required for each person in the RV weekly.

I laughed, thanked him for his time and moved on to my second option.

There was no way we were going to agree to work 60 hours each week just for the site. I found this to be an employer's kid tax initiative, which led me to believe his property was not as family friendly as he made it seem.

I also use this same judgment when traveling, for campgrounds who charge additional rates for children without amenities or anything more than a gravel parking spot.

I caution you against agreeing to such a situation, as you will not be getting a fair trade.

TOP 7 MYTHS & MISTAKES

With anything that involves a variety of people with a variety of opinions, workamping is best known for some of the most inaccurate information!

Preconceived notions about what it is and what it isn't are quickly followed by a host of common myths that are almost always trailed by a big mistake!

In this chapter, we will dive into the top workamping myths and mistakes that you should know and avoid.

MYTH #1: ALL JOBS ARE SIMILAR

Several types of workamping jobs may seem similar on the surface. Working as a park host at one State Park over another may seem like a simple decision, but in fact, the two jobs can be uniquely different.

Each job will have its own unique destination and that alone is worth doing research to look into whether the location is somewhere you want to spend a month, a season, or longer.

Other differences can be the pay, job responsibilities, benefits, use of on-site amenities and even the community or lack of one, regarding other RVers living on-site.

Mistake #1: Taking the First Job Offered.

Once you've done all the planning and prep to actually make it possible to get on the road, you can easily lose yourself in taking the very first position that is offered to you. This is the biggest mistake a working RVer can make.

Not only are you literally not giving yourself a chance to grab the best possible position, but you're also probably not giving yourself time to think over the details of this specific job opportunity and what exactly it entails.

Do not take the first job you are offered. It is likely glowing and looks amazing simply because it's the first job being offered. Do yourself a favor and take some time, a day or more, to think it over completely.

If the employer cannot wait for you to make sure this job is something you can wholeheartedly commit to, then this employer is not someone who you will want to work for.

MYTH #2: FREE = TRADE FOR HOURS WORKED

Some RV employers will ask for a specific number of hours to cover your site rent. While this is a common practice, it is not the equivalent to providing a FHU.

Working 20, 10 or even 2 hours to cover the cost of your site, is not free regardless of how you spin it.

Make sure if you agree to work for your 'FREE site' that you calculate the number of hours you're working for it and see how much exactly you are being asked to pay.

Mistake #2: Pay Top Dollar For A Free Site.

Let's be very clear, a free site is one that costs you nothing and requires no hours worked in exchange. Working for your site or paying more than what a typical guest would be asked to pay is both wrong and underhanded on the part of the employer.

RVers should never have to pay a daily rate multiplied by 30 days in a month for their site.

They should be provided a monthly or seasonal rate even if one is not publicly available. RVers should also not be asked to trade more hours than would amount to the monthly or seasonal rate divided by their rate of pay, or minimum wage at the very least.

Since some employers are hiring RVers to help the bottom line, they can sometimes forget entirely about how valuable your time and efforts are, not to mention the added bonus of hiring people who are skilled and have life experience.

When accepting and/or reviewing positions, make sure you do your homework! Break out the calculator and put a dollar sign to your site to make sure it's free or at least fair.

MYTH #3: TRUST EVERY AD

Employment ads for RVers are no different from employment ads for other jobs.

They are designed to highlight the good and reel you in as an applicant. Employers are looking for people to fill positions and some will overextend themselves in an effort to do so (that's putting it nicely).

Every ad you read is created to attract RVers to apply and inquire further about the position. They should never be read as 'cut and dry'. These ads require further investigation to obtain pertinent details you will want to have before driving any distance!

Mistake #3: Not Doing Your Research.

You have to do your own research!

Read as many TripAdvisor reviews, blog posts, workamping job review posts as you can find. You can also do a thorough read of the employer's website to give you a good overview of the business and possibly what it's like to visit and/or work at the location.

"You need this information to make your decision!"

Now I know everyone has an opinion and that we don't always agree on things, but there is something to be said about hearing from past guests as well as past employees what you are getting into.

You don't have to use this as your sole decision-making reference point but read through and have some information on the back burner for when you do!

MYTH #4: WORKAMPING DOESN'T PAY

Many employers that hire RVers are looking to get the most bang for their buck. As a result, they will advertise low wages for these jobs and some might even require more hours worked in exchange for a site than you are comfortable working.

But this is not the case for all RV employers!

In fact, there are more and more companies finding their groove with the Live Camp Work community and have found that compared to the local employment pool, RVers are higher value even if you pay for all hours and give them a FREE site.

Mistake #4: Undervaluing Yourself.

Never underestimate the value of your contributions! Your time and your work are worth something, and they're likely worth way more than you think!

Employers are thinking about themselves, for the most part, when they set their starting wages for new hires.

You should do the same!

Think about what you are bringing to the table and how you will contribute to the overall success of this business.

Now do your homework and decide what your bottom dollar figure is and stick to it.

You should be able to negotiate at the very least the benefits that come along with the position you are accepting, if for some reason you are not able to get them to wiggle on the price per hour.

MYTH #5: MULTIPLE SEASONS ARE BEST

Working RVers might think that committing to multiple seasons with an employer is the best way to secure a position. While this is not entirely wrong, as many employers would love to hire for multiple seasons at one time, it isn't the only way to make sure you have jobs lined up for each season.

Mistake #5: Getting Stuck In A Travel Cycle.

Workamping is about travel and working along the way... You're not doing much traveling and exploring if you continuously rotate between the same two or three jobs.

I know this is super easy to plan and coordinate, especially with reliable jobs from big employers like Amazon, but it definitely leaves you stuck in a rut on a rotation that misses probably the best part of the lifestyle... freedom of location!

Before you schedule yourself for multiple seasons or multiple years at the same RV employer, consider venturing out and seeking something new.

You might enjoy seeing different destinations and partaking in different aspects of workamping. At the very least try not to repeat half of your jobs for any given year.

MYTH #6: ALL WORK & NO PLAY

Repeatedly we hear someone in the crowd say "workamping? I don't want to work!" And to be honest this probably is not the ticket to travel for them. Working along the way is one of the best ways to hit the road now!

It is the single reason so many people in America have been able to travel full-time. Workamping involves work. Real work. It's a main component of the lifestyle that leads to other amazing benefits, such as the ability to travel!

Mistake #6: Not Taking Time To Explore.

Some folks do get caught up in the working part of workamping. They find a job they enjoy and go hard at being the best. These are the RVers that employers dream about. But sometimes these folks do not make time for exploring locally, which I feel is the biggest mistake!

We should all put our best foot forward and do so without hesitation wearing a big smile, but with work ethics in consideration remember why you started workamping. For most of us, it will be for the adventures rather than the job. Make sure you don't just sleep on your days off!

Take this time to get out into the surrounding area and explore! Find adventures both big and small around every corner and you will enjoy workamping 110% more than you thought!

MYTH #7: APPLY, INTERVIEW & DONE

I wish it were that simple! But there is more to acquiring a good workamping position than simply filling out an application and completing an interview.

Some employers will want more than one interview, others will want to verify past employment and do background checks. Some will want pictures of you and your rig, others will ask for a virtual meet & greet.

Workamping jobs are similar to those you've likely worked in the past, as in

each employer will have his/her own way of doing things and you have to roll with it if you are serious about getting the job!

Mistake #7: Not Getting It In Writing.

A big mistake many RVers both new and seasoned make, is not getting a signed work agreement for each position they accept.

Phone interviews and friendly verbal agreements are great, but when you are traveling, sometimes thousands of miles, you want to make sure everyone is on the same page!

There's just no room for mistakes and miscommunications. So if you will go one step further and make sure you have all the details of your arrangement in writing, you can bet on a better experience every time.

Of course, I can't say for sure this will alleviate all chances of having an issue after arrival with what is expected vs. what was discussed but having a signed agreement with what you've agreed to will help refresh anyone's mind who's confused, forgotten or dismissed certain details!

Start up a conversation at a campfire with a group of working RVers and you'll quickly find out workamping is not for everyone.

To be honest, it takes a special kind of person to enjoy the RV lifestyle in general, so once you add in the fact that you will be working along the way, well…. let's just say you're bound to find a soul or two that have had a less than desirable experience.

Use the information we just covered to help you avoid falling into this group of folks who have a salty aftertaste of the workamping lifestyle and may have missed their chance to ever truly enjoy it!

FINDING THE JOBS

By definition, workamping is all about work and travel. Both pieces are equally important, but for some the work leads to the travel, thus making it a higher priority.

Some people make a conscious choice to just work one season and use the remaining months of the year for exploration and personal adventures. Others will work season to season and find time to explore along the way and in the surrounding areas.

However you decide it's best to structure your RV lifestyle, make sure you know how to get the jobs that fit your needs and your wants. With so many different employers offering jobs to the RV community, sometimes it can be hard to figure out how to t go about applying for them, interviewing, and even how to negotiate the compensation you feel is appropriate for your time and skills.

You can give yourself a leg up by knowing a few things before you make your first step towards obtaining these jobs. Let's take a look.

BE PREPARED

Once you've made the decision to head out on the road, the only thing holding you back is finding that perfect job, right?

To get the job, you have to be prepared with tools and information that will help you make the right impression from your first point of contact.

First, you'll want to know your personal boundaries. These are the things you will and will not do, what type of compensation you are looking for, and where you are willing to travel.

Armed with this information, you'll be able to negotiate your compensation with almost every employer you encounter. You will know what job duties you are comfortable doing and what things you just aren't willing to compromise on. For some people, this is cleaning toilets and for others, it's using a computer for reservations. Everyone is different, so choose your boundaries and stick to them.

Most employers will request a resume and having your outline of past jobs will make it easy for you to create one. Don't be afraid to list your prior skills in lifelong careers, these skills are tried and true and you can use many of them in workamping jobs depending on what positions you are applying for.

MAKE A CONNECTION

Think back to those corporate interviews - do you remember the type of questions they asked you?

These are the same questions RV employers will ask you, so please be prepared.

When you apply to a position, do some research on the company. Pull up everything you can on their RV jobs program and check out reviews posted by others who have worked for them.

"Give yourself the ultimate leg up by being prepared…"

then be ready for the interview where you'll need to connect with the employer to seal the deal.

Because you'll likely not be able to meet with the employer in-person, you will do all of your interviews with employers over the phone or via apps

like Skype and FaceTime. Now is not the time to be shy or timid. Be you! Let your personality shine through.

Employers are looking for people who can communicate with them and form an instant bond.

If you cannot connect with the employer over the phone, there is a really good chance you will not be called for a second interview and ultimately won't get the job. Your voice should show your personality and you should describe your skillset in a conversational tone without being pushy, brash, or interrupting.

STAND OUT

Find a way to stand out if you really want the job!

With thousands of other RVers out there, the best tip anyone can give you is to find a way to set yourself apart from the masses.

What makes you the best bet for the employer? Why should they invest their time and money into training you to do a job with their company? What can you offer that sets you ahead of the competition?

These are the questions you need to have the answers to prior to applying for your first workamping job. Think about these questions! Sit down and take some time to really plan out good answers that you can confidently convey to the employer during your interview!

BUILD A NETWORK

There is something to be said about the ability to network in the RV community. Although many would disagree that it's necessary to get a job, I think we can all agree that having a solid network of contacts can make finding jobs easier by having one foot in the door!

I'm not saying that you have to be the social media king or queen and participate in every RV Facebook group discussion. But I am going to encourage you to get out of your comfort zone and talk to the interesting people you meet along the way! Building a network organically and naturally will serve you much better down the road than just inviting everyone to be your friend or follow you online!

Many RVers proclaim their ability to acquire jobs just based on 'who you know'. If this is the case, it's better to play it safe and have a few contacts in your back pocket for a rainy day.

9 STEPS TO GETTING A JOB

Using the following steps will help you gain confidence in your workamping job search.

While each step is not necessarily hard to complete, they are each equally important and will take some time to accomplish. Researching employers isn't always the most fun task, but you will be glad you did.

Step 1: Pick a Location.

Decide which states you want to work in for the period of time you want to work. If you have an idea of specific areas within the state, that's even better.

Have a short list of at least 3-5 states to start, but please know the more options you give yourself, the better chances you have of finding work.

Step 2: Create a Resume.

You will have to send a resume to apply for 99.9% of the jobs advertised, so you might as well get started and create one. Remember, workamping resumes are a general resume that focuses on highlighting your skill set and the workamping jobs you've had in the past. One resume is usually fine whether you are a couple, family, or solo worker.

Step 3: Apply ASAP!

As soon as you see a new job posted, you need to apply! Do not wait until later. Do not wait until that night or that afternoon. Send them your resume right then.

Employers are bombarded with emails for these jobs, so the quicker you get your resume emailed, the higher up it will be in the stack. At some point they will stop looking at new resumes in their inbox; you need to make sure yours is already submitted by this point!

Step 4: Research the Employer

It's easy to read an attractive advertisement and instantly think that this is the job for you! But how much do you really know about this employer and this opportunity?

Make sure you take some time to research the employer, read reviews about their RV program and their property in general.

If guests can't stand to be there, chances are you won't be able to either!

Do your homework!

Step 5: Wait 1-3 Days to Follow Up.

If you think employers will email you back, you're about 50% right. But as you can see, the odds are pretty risky - don't take the chance. Follow up on each job you apply for within one to three days of sending your initial interest. Call (if they provided a phone number in their ad) or send a quick email to see if they are still accepting applications/resumes and if the position is still open. Let them know you are very interested in the position and would love the opportunity to set up an interview!

Step 6: Nail the Interview!

You have one shot to get this right!

When the employer asks, "Are you available for an interview at ___." Your answer should always be "Yes!" And while this isn't always possible, do everything in your power to avoid saying no.

> *"You need to make it easy for them to choose you."*

Once on the phone, show your personality and talk about how your skills will help their business. Don't go overboard, but really sell yourself! The first interview is the most important as it will either lead to the next step or sometimes seal the deal right away.

Step 7: Negotiate.

You don't have to say yes to the first thing they offer you. Know your worth and find a way to negotiate the things you want/need to be able to happily complete your commitment.

If the pay is low, ask for something higher. If the perks are blah, see if you can get your site for free or have use of park amenities like a golf cart or kayak. Find things to negotiate to make it worth your while.

You'll thank yourself later!

Step 8: Get It In Writing.

The worst thing you can do is set up a great job and not get the details in writing.

This is called a Work Agreement and you should try to get one for every job you accept. I recommend never traveling to a new job without a detailed description of your job duties, the start and end dates, arrival information, compensation, extra perks, and end-of-season information.

Do yourself a favor and ask each RV employer to send a Work Agreement clearly detailing these items, if nothing more than just for peace-of-mind. This is not a contract per se, but a tool you can use to help get things back on the right track if issues arise during the season.

Step 9: Confirm Before You Travel!

Before you pack up and embark on your road trip to your new job, make sure you email or call the employer to confirm your date of arrival.

Never assume that nothing has changed since your last conversation, especially if it was months ago. Confirm the details with your next employer within the same week you plan to travel.

SECTION 2

WAYS OF WORKAMPING

There are many ways of workamping and I'm sure you'll find your groove with at least a few programs that fit your needs and suit your travels.

So, forget about fixing your desired schedule to fit that of your current employer... forget about starting on a date that is determined and desired by someone other than yourself... forget about doing a job you don't really want to do for a wage that you really feel is unfair.

With positions, compensation, and employers just as flexible as your travels, finding a job that suits all your needs is completely within reach. In fact, it's more likely you'll have a harder time choosing which job to accept and which jobs to postpone until the next year.

Workamping employers have the flexibility to structure and create their programs as they see fit. Some will offer career type benefits with a 401K and health insurance others will stick to the norm and just provide an hourly wage and a free FHU (full hook-up). It's up to you to decide if their location, compensation and job opportunities are a good fit for your travels and lifestyle.

In this section, I'd like to take a detailed look into several popular RV programs as well as Campground Jobs in general!

CAMPGROUND & RV PARK JOBS

Before you start searching for jobs, take a minute to learn the details of the most popular type of workamping operation, their typical compensation packages and the popular positions available...

I'm talking about Campgrounds & RV Parks!

CAMPGROUND TYPES

Knowing the types of campgrounds & RV parks looking to hire RVers is a must for anyone looking for work while traveling. There are many other types of businesses that hire RVers too, but if working in a campground excites you, this will help narrow your search when looking for employment.

Let's look at three types and discuss the general idea of each.

Multi-Park Corporations:

You're likely familiar with names like Kampgrounds of America (KOA), Equity Lifestyle Properties, Forever Resorts, and Jellystone Parks, but others like Sky Valley Resorts and Cal-Am Resorts also fall into the multi-park category.

These entities operate campgrounds in multiple states which provides RVers with a "wherever you want to go next" kind of freedom.

Though some of these resorts may have individual owner-operators, there will still be corporate or franchise rules and regulations to follow.

Typically, working for one of these larger entities will include some paid hours instead of just working in trade for an RV site. Due to the size of some of these parks, many RVers enjoy creating a community of like-minded co-workers with multiple RVers being hired at each location and sometimes in the same positions.

Private Parks:

Many jobs are offered by private individuals who own a small business that benefit from hiring RVers who can relate better to their guests than other local hires. Often with individually-owned or family-run operations, you will become "part of the family" during your season there.

Each owner will have their own unique way of running their business, which you may or may not agree with.

Dealing with "small town politics" isn't for everyone, and you hopefully won't find it at every park. If you can learn to work around those situations and maintain a positive attitude, then working for a private owner will open the flood gates with a steady stream of job opportunities.

Government-Run:

Workamping at one of the many government-run parks can offer the ability to see new and exciting parts of the country from an insider's perspective, while being entrenched in the natural beauty of the great outdoors.

Living on-site in these more scenic parks is completely different from a quick weekend road trip, offering more time to explore the surrounding area.

With these types of RV parks, you can negotiate shorter-term commitments. This differs from most commercial campgrounds, which prefer you work for an entire summer or winter season.

Government entities post job listings for multiple positions and time frames via volunteer.gov, their own city, and on their county or state's website.

Examples of government run parks are state parks, county parks, U.S. Army Corps of Engineer campgrounds, and U.S. Forest Service campgrounds. RVers in these parks are considered seasonal hires of volunteers, since they are most often working a minimal number of hours for an RV site (which may or may not have full hookups).

These entities rely on the volunteers to keep the facility open and running, so RVers often feel a more genuine appreciation for their work. And while many positions post ads strictly for volunteers, it is good to know that some will offer their volunteers a small stipend or expense reimbursements.

COMPENSATION PACKAGES

Knowing the different types of compensation offered will give you a better idea of which jobs you should apply to. If you know these three main types of compensations, you'll know how and where to start your negotiations.

Knowing what the offer means beforehand will make sure you understand the work agreement prior to accepting the job.

Work For Site:

Working for your RV site is a great option for someone with an additional stream of income. Many campgrounds offer these arrangements in hopes of finding RVers who are not relying on a paycheck and come instead for the beautiful scenery or exciting locale, along with a few hours a week of busy work.

Employers will offer a job in exchange for your site by stating something similar to this: "FHU for 12 hours per week."

FHU + All Hours Paid:

The most desirable compensation agreement is one in which the employer will pay you for all hours worked at a specified rate PLUS include an RV site with hookups.

An employment ad might say: "FHU provided plus $10.50/hour for all hours worked. 30 hours/week."

This is a very attractive deal for the RVer, because all their living expenses would be included, and as a result, these jobs would typically be the first off the market.

Make sure to apply early and put your best foot forward. They'll have many applicants to consider and you will likely have just one chance to pitch yourself!

Combination Package:

In some cases, the employer will agree to pay for all hours but requires you to pay a reduced rate for your site.

Or they may require a set number of hours each week to cover the cost of the site and utilities. This compromise is considered a combination package. Either you get paid for all hours and you pay for your site, or you work for the site and get paid for the additional hours.

An example of this compensation would be an ad reading: "FHU for 12 hours, all others paid at $9/hour".

Words of advice: Make sure you have a written agreement that states the actual number of hours you'll work after the site is "paid for," or you could end up just working for your site.

CAMPGROUND POSITIONS

Now that you know the kinds of campgrounds and compensation out there, you may be wondering what jobs tend to be most available?

Popular workamping positions are just a starting point for your RV travels. Work is available all across the map in just about every job category you can think of but looking at what's most commonly offered at campgrounds will give you an idea of what to expect for this type of operation in particular.

Campground Host:

This was the original RV job and as more and more people entered the lifestyle, more and more employers, including private, government run campgrounds have started to hire campground hosts for their properties!

> *"Campground hosting is the most iconic workamping job you can get."*

The idea of living on-site while welcoming fellow campers, answering questions, escorting, and closing the park gates are some basic job functions and picture perfect for many folks living the RV life.

Less strenuous labor requirements, the ability to (usually) work from your site, and the opportunity to return year after year make these positions highly sought after.

Front Desk/Office Staff:

Along with the comforts of working mostly indoors with air conditioning, the job of the front desk staff is quite appealing for those who know their way around the computer. Entering reservations, checking out customers on a POS system, answering phones and assisting with customer questions and requests are the main responsibilities for this position.

Standing on your feet with little movement can be a downside, but based on your property location, this might not be an issue. Many front desk associates have a background in customer service or retail that serves them well for these jobs.

But, even a newbie to computer reservations can pick up most park software relatively quickly with the right amount of training and support.

Activity Director:

As the most organized person on the campground staff, the Activity Director has to be well equipped with a Plan A, B & C at all times.

Responsible for recreation, events, activities and the overall fun-factor of the property, you have to know your property, plan accordingly, and make sure each activity or event is structured and staffed to ensure guests enjoy themselves.

A typical day can include hours of computer work, researching crafts and creating themed games, as well as training the recreation staff on how to properly conduct the activities and then, of course, actually overseeing the events throughout the property.

Housekeeping:

Housekeeping is one of those love-it-or-leave-it positions. If you love what you do and you're good at it, then you'll enjoy it. If you don't, then just leave it alone.

> *"the hardest workamping job at most properties."*

Cleaning cabins, washing laundry, keeping up the bath houses and the main buildings like the office and cafe is hard work. It's made even harder by the necessity to redo the work throughout the day because the spaces may be heavily utilized.

Maintenance:

This is one of those jobs that no matter how much you do and how many employees are working together, there will always be something else that pops up. The job of property maintenance is never ending. From sun up to sun down, there are jobs in different areas that will require attention.

Some will be more pressing than others, but all will need to be completed ASAP. Typical duties can range from cleaning fire rings, to mowing lawns, to installing electrical in new cabins over the winter. Based on your experience, certifications, level of comfort and expertise, taking a job in property maintenance can mean a lot of different things.

THE REALITY

Workamping jobs come in all shapes and sizes... just like the adventurous people who apply for them! They are easily customized to meet the needs of the masses, making them perfect for you, your neighbor and your friend down the road.

It is in your best interest to negotiate each and every agreement with employers to make sure you are getting the best experience in return for your hard work and dedication.

THE SUGAR BEET HARVEST

Sit around a warm campfire from Winter to late Fall with a group of fellow RVers and you're bound to hear at least one story from an adventurous soul who worked the Sugar Beet Harvest last year.

Listen to the energized rants about freezing temperatures, weather-based days off and the exhausting 12-hour shifts that seemed to never end! Then pay close attention to the climax as the story shifts to a tale of a once in a lifetime experience, the beautiful friendships that were made, and the greatest pay in the shortest amount of time for any workamping job.

Now sit back and relax as groups of fellow RVers chime in on how they plan to make the trip to North Dakota & Minnesota this year for the exact same thing!

OVERVIEW

The annual migration starts after the end of the summer camping season, when Labor Day celebrations are just dwindling down. RVers who have hunkered down in the top tourist destinations of the year, now make their way South, heading for snowbird approved destinations for the Fall & Winter months ahead. The highways are packed with RVers heading south and far west, but many RVers have a different idea.

Easy to spot, since they might seem to be headed in the wrong direction, as they steadily drive farther north with their hearts set on racking in big cash before calling it quits for the year!

They've signed an agreement with Express Employment Professionals to work the Sugar Beet Harvest, what some call an Unbeatable Experience.

Committing usually for the full month of October, give or take a few days depending on mother nature's plan for the weather that year, they stand to rack in about $2500 a piece for just 2 weeks of work.

The Sugar Beet Harvest is championed by a collective effort between Express Employment Professionals who hires for the nation's two largest sugar producers, American Crystal Sugars and Sidney Sugars.

Together they actively hire more than 1500 employees to work the harvest each year at 42 receiving stations and 6 factories.

Since the local unemployment rate is pretty much non-existent, meaning everyone who wants to work is already working, RVers are seen by some as the reliable infantry of seasonal help for the booming 5-billion-dollar beet industry.

In fact, if you're a numbers person, you might be surprised, or at least interested to know that a whopping 42% of these 1500+ positions are filled by RVers each year!

Americans love their sugar!

And while working the Sugar Beet is a unique workamping experience, the hiring team likes to be upfront and honest about the details of this opportunity to ensure that RVers are making the best decision for their personal situations when deciding if this opportunity is right for them.

Express Employment makes it *crystal clear* that these positions and this experience "is not for everybody" so make sure you read on and do your due diligence to gather all the information before submitting your application for this year's harvest.

AVAILABLE POSITIONS

There are a variety of positions for folks interested in the Harvest! This year alone, they have 160 positions at their Montana location and almost 800 at the locations in the Red River Valley. With that said, many RVers make this seasonal commitment a reoccurring staple in their working arsenal before hunkering down for the Winter. So naturally, almost 400 of those are already spoken for by the almost 50% of returning RVers.

The following is a list of 3 major hiring categories for the harvest.

Helper/Sample Taker:

These are the general job positions RVers are being hired for. The majority of applicants will be hired for these jobs, as this is the only position Express Employment can guarantee placement for.

Basic job responsibilities may include collecting beet samples and assisting the Piler Operators in cleaning and maintaining the area. Helpers will also communicate with drivers to ensure safe and accurate unloading of the delivery trucks.

Quality Lab:

6 indoor positions are offered inside the Quality Lab, where samples are tested to determine the farmer's pay for their crops: Dock, Tare, Scale, Brei Belt, Brei Mixer & LDB Quality.

While these positions are all indoors and only require 10-hour shifts, positions in the Quality Lab are very limited, still require constant standing and are a very important part of the harvest operation. RVers who wish to secure these jobs, are urged to apply as early as possible.

Skilled Positions:

There are a limited amount of skilled labor positions available each year.

Each will require past knowledge and operation skills of heavy equipment and applicants will be hand selected by American Sugars.

Returning RVers who have proven their reliability and great work ethic are more likely to be accepted into these positions after year 1 is complete. If you are interested in these positions, send your resume along with your online application and be prepared for an onsite 'audition' once you are in the area.

Piler Operator: Maneuvers the piler control switches, orchestrates repair work, supervises and assists in the cleanup of daily operations.

Skid Steer Operator: Places deep freeze pipes and helps clean and maintain the pile area.

WORKING CONDITIONS

As you can probably image, the working conditions of the Sugar Beet Harvest will be drastically different from the cozy campground store you might have worked in last Summer.

The luxury of sitting for hours on end, chatting with guests about the crowding at the pool and installation of the new sauna should not be compared to the sights and sounds of working the harvest

This is not a job you accept based on the beautiful view from your campsite, the perks of using the employee golf carts or the ability to explore the local area for new experiences.

HOW CAN I PREPARE FOR THIS?

Working the Sugar Beet Harvest is a strenuous workamping job that will require some preparation prior to your arrival. During the summer prior to your harvest experience, it is advisable to add daily exercises like jogging, swimming, yoga, Pilates, stretching, and/or light weightlifting to your health regimen. Preparing your body for physically demanding work can help lighten the harshness of the physicality you'll experience after arrival.

Start by slowly implementing exercise into your daily habits and grow to include more over the full course of the summer.

Even small efforts like walking your dog more often and for longer periods or riding a bike to the store instead of driving will pay off in the long run!

THINGS TO KNOW BEFORE YOU GO

- The Sugar Beet Harvest is relatively short, at just about 10-14 working days.
- The pay is good and starts at $13/hr. Increases are given to returning workers who come back for consecutive seasons and those in skilled labor positions.
- Shifts are long and span a full 12 hours in most cases, during which you will spend most of your time on your feet.
- Your campsite is provided FREE as part of your compensation package, and you will not receive a 1099 at the end of the

year or see the value noted on your pay stubs.
- The first 8 hours of your shift are paid at the regular pay rate, while the last 4 are paid at time and a half.
- Saturdays are paid at time and a half and they offer Sundays at either time and a half or double time- depending on the location.
- Temperatures drop below freezing usually during the nights, so all employees will need to be prepared to work throughout their entire shift wearing the appropriate layered clothing.
- Operations can shut down on days when it's too hot, too cold or too wet.
- When you complete your agreed commitment, you will receive a 5% Harvest Completion Bonus as an extra thank you for your hard work and dedication to seeing the project through!
- Basic job requirements require that everyone must be able to lift a minimum of 25lbs.

CAMPGROUND INFORMATION

Working with 32 Campgrounds in the region, part of your compensation will include your campsite.

Once hired on, the HR Staff will make your reservations and take care of all the details including paying for the site.

It was said by the Express team, that not all campgrounds are created equal. The sooner you get your application in, the better your chances of getting a spot at one of the nicer ones.

Most of the Campgrounds they offer provide a full hook up.

If you by chance get a campground without sewer, they will offer a honey wagon service free of charge. Also, if the temperature drops and the campgrounds have to shut off the water at the campsite, which has only really happened during the very last part of October when the season stretched out, they would provide a water truck also free of charge to fill your tanks.

Some campgrounds will have a campground host on site, but not all are able to offer this amenity.

Most of the campgrounds are located very near to towns with gas stations, groceries, laundromats and hardware stores. But heading to Walmart and other big box stores would require more driving and possibly a shutdown day for enough time and energy to make the trip.

They do ask that RVers arrive with enough propane and food rations to allow for two full weeks of work without requiring an errand trip to go get more, just in case.

The farthest campground is about 28 miles away from the piling site, so make sure you have a reliable vehicle or transportation to get to and from work, as walking would not be an option.

Most sites are said to be about a 10-minute commute to work, which isn't bad and for RVers without a tow or in town vehicle, carpooling with friendly neighbors is always an option.

CLOTHING TIPS

Temperatures range between cool and windy to dropping below freezing especially during the nights, so you have to anticipate the need to layer your clothing. I can't imagine anything worse than working a 12-hour shift feeling unprepared and uncomfortable in a miscalculated wardrobe choice I could have prevented.

Plan to layer your clothing for all shifts! You can always take a layer off if you get hot but trying to find an extra sweater lying around in a pile of beets, I can only imagine would be quite difficult.

Insulated gloves, multiple pairs of broken-in boots, a few insoles or heated liners, thermal underwear, snow pants, heavy jackets, face masks, beanies, and hoodies are all recommended essentials!

The consensus seems to be that you should make a big trip to the thrift store for clothing you don't expect to ever wear again! Apparently, the smell of Sugar Beets isn't all that great and once the dirt gets on you, its stuck!

HIRING PROCESS

- Submit online or by paper application, which they will mail to you.
- They will contact you for more information and to discuss details to move forward.
- Contact from your point person every 30-45 days leading up to the harvest.
- Arrival dates and campground assignment will be given after July 4th

CONTACT DETAILS

Web: www.sugarbeetharvest.com

Phone: (888) 791-6738

AMAZON'S CAMPERFORCE

Working for the online super giant is truly an experience that's hard to put into words.

There are so many pieces to the story that need to be told and there is usually very little time to tell it. To be honest, working at Amazon can best be described as working for a well-oiled machine. I know that sounds cliché, but it's true.

Everything from the moment you step inside the building is planned, timed, scheduled, organized and then constantly being tracked, measured and observed for ways to make it better and more efficient.

Working in one of their fulfillment centers, inside the Camperforce program, means working for one of the largest, if not the largest, online retailer in the World. You're on the inside and you'll soon see first-hand what happens after a customer makes a purchase from their computer screen.

You're working day in and day out to fill orders not only for customers, but

most likely for your family members as well. Time is everything and your 'numbers' will show how your performance rates against the typical Amazon employee.

A TYPICAL DAY

A typical day depends on which department you're working in, the number of orders to be filled and what shift you're working on.

Generally, you'll clock in after entering the building and dropping off personal items in your locker. Clocking in for the day is a sight to see! Employees line up at every time clock and wait patiently for the exact second when their shift begins. Then one by one they scan their badges and proceed to their start areas.

After arriving at your start-up area you will meet with your department heads at a start-up meeting, where basic stretches are done as a group, while important information is relayed through your Manager.

After setting off to your station, or if you're a Picker– wherever your scanner directs you, your day will progress until either a scheduled break, lunch or the end of your shift.

Throughout the day, there is limited time to socialize with fellow campers or employees (unless of course you're a Picker) but making time for a quick "How's it going?" will help you maintain your sanity after hours and hours of repetition and checking your productivity.

At the end of your shift, you'll again notice an extremely long line of campers and employees at each time clock. As they wait for the clock to tick– conversations about 'work' and 'numbers' fill the air until the exact moment their badges touch the scanner and they exit the building!

FIRST THINGS FIRST

For first time applicants the application and hiring process for the Camperforce program can be long, drawn out and filled with delayed responses.

From the moment you submit your resume or online application, wheels will naturally begin moving in your head. You're ready to go! Right? Well, not so fast. When they say Application Process, they really mean it.

I would allow at least a month lead time from start to finish, and more likely 2-3 months, but then again, some folks get hired in just a few weeks, so you never really know.

There are hundreds of applicants sending in their resumes and only a small on-site staff of HR personnel to sort through them all. Give them some time and just plan on waiting a few days between emails and sometimes even up to a week in-between step. They do an amazing job of getting pretty much everyone who wants to work placed into a position!

APPLICATION PROCESS:

- Fill out the online application on the Amazon Camperforce website.
- Provide proof of education (transcripts/diploma/degree). You must be a High School Graduate or equivalent.
- Pass Background Test & Drug Screening
- Start Date Given, based on the date you stated you are available.
- Pre-Employment Paperwork: Forms, needing to be completed prior to your start date.
- Orientation consists of a few hours of Amazon policies and protocols and can be followed

by a few hours of training inside the fulfillment center, so wear sneakers!

KNOWING WHAT TO EXPECT

Even if this is your first time, you really do need to know what to expect. You should know what you're signing up for.

Reading every review available will give you information, both good and bad. Just try to keep an open mind and pull from each personal story whatever information is given about the job, the available positions, the workload, the schedules, typical days, location information, community details and the expectations for Camperforce Associates.

Take notes on what you've gathered and transform these notes into questions.

Once you're called for your phone interview, make sure to refer to your questions for the information you need to know. You can also bring up any last minute or unanswered questions at orientation or in a quick email to the HR Staff at the site you've decided is best for you.

"The first year I did Camperforce, I really did have a horrible time."

I dreaded waking up at 5 a.m. every day to go to a job I chose, only to realize I didn't like it. I had no idea what working in a warehouse was like. I had never even seen a conveyor system and barely knew what a tote was.

As I looked around at all the smiling campers having a great time, I couldn't figure out what I had done wrong! Then it hit me - this wasn't what I signed up for. I signed up to fill customer orders in a fulfillment center. This was not what I had in mind!

If you think about my first experience, you've probably already noticed - this wasn't Amazon's fault.

It was actually my own. I hadn't asked many questions when I agreed to take the position. I was excited and let that excitement overtake my rationale to ask any probing questions.

I had no warehouse experience, but I never once asked what a typical day inside the fulfillment center would entail.

BEING PREPARED

Going into this job with the notion that you'll just "wing it," is the worst mistake an RVer could make.

Showing up to a campground to work in the store or maybe reservations for the summer may be something to "just wing." However, signing up to work at Amazon during their Peak Season, when millions of holiday orders are being pumped out at the very last minute, is something you should prepare for.

When I left Camperforce in 2013, I swore up and down, I would never return.

Then after about a year, I started thinking... maybe I should give it another chance. After all, my horrible experience was largely the effect of my own lack of preparation. If I knew what to expect, I could have prepared. And if I prepared, I would've had a really great time just like the other RVers.

Working in a warehouse is mentally and physically draining, so preparing for your job with the Camperforce program will require exercise prior to your arrival.

In the weeks and months prior to your start date, I recommend you slowly increase your physical activity level and try to walk as much and as often as possible.

Training your body for long periods of movement and even just standing for extended periods of time will help you adjust easier to life inside the fulfillment center.

In addition to physical labor, mental stamina will also be a major factor since employee safety is such a major concern.

There are procedures and required protocols for just about every action you make and every job you will perform. You need to be constantly aware of your surroundings, as well as your own actions to make sure you're upholding the high level of safety Amazon expects at each of its locations.

Preparing yourself both mentally and physically will make transitioning into your new role a whole lot smoother.

TOP 3 JOB PICKS

There are three main positions that Amazon has been known to hire RVers for over the years.

These positions are responsible for, as Amazon Camperforce Representatives say, "Getting the right product, into the right box and shipped to the right customer, every time!"

The positions are known as pick, pack and stow. Let's take a look!

Stow: (v) to put into a place for storage.

Ex.) Employees will stow merchandise into their assigned bins within the fulfillment center.

When merchandise is received in the fulfillment center, the associates in the Stowing Department have the job of making sure it reaches the shelves not only in a timely manner, but also with the correct labels and into the correct bin so that Pickers can retrieve the items with relative ease.

Stowers typically walk between 5-8 miles per day.

Pick: (v) to choose from a group.

Ex.) Make sure to pick the exact item, as described on your scanner to avoid mistakes.

After products have been stowed properly, Pickers receive bin locations on their scanners, report to that location, and ultimately retrieve the correct product with 100% accuracy.

The Picking Department is the largest department, involves the most walking (ranging between 8-12 miles per day) and makes up the majority of available jobs for Camperforce.

Pack: (v) to put into or arrange compactly.

Ex.) Pack your items securely by using cello to fill your boxes before applying the label.

The Packing Department waits for the filled totes to arrive at their stations on conveyor belts. They then sort and pack the items into boxes to fulfill specific customer orders.

Packing requires less walking than the above two departments, but physical activity is still required.

THE RUN DOWN

At the close of the traditional camping season, many RVers find themselves in search of a quick gig before heading south or west for the winter.

Keeping everything, we've already discussed in mind, I consider working for Camperforce to be a great option for many RVers including singles, couples, and even families. Amazon does a great job at accommodating all types of travelers, and with several positions, locations and schedules available, there's sure to be something that will suit your needs.

Who

Just about anyone and everyone can work the Camperforce program. People of all ages and backgrounds in all different rigs, campers and RVs. If you're relatively healthy, over the age of 18, able to pass a drug screening and background test and you have a 'recreation vehicle', you'll probably be hired. Check the website for exact details.

What

Camperforce is all about working in one of the nation's largest online retailer's warehouses. Amazon calls them fulfillment centers, but in an attempt to clarify, I'll make it clear-you will be working in an extremely large warehouse (possibly the size of a small village) with all the pros and cons that it entails.

Where

Camperforce is available at select fulfillment centers throughout the US. In 2015 there were four centers recruiting for the Peak season. Jeffersonville, IN, Campbellsville, KY, Murfreesboro, TN or Haslet, TX. Last time I spoke with a Camperforce representative, they were actively hiring for 6 locations all on the east coast. Check online for specific locations and to apply for these positions.

When

Typically, the Camperforce season starts sometime in early to mid-August running through Thanksgiving ending right before Christmas. Recently, the Camperforce program expanded their locations and the dates of the program, allowing for not only longer employment if desired, but also a range of dates and the ability to work at multiple sites back to back.

Why

Holiday orders of course! Camperforce is the brainchild that allows Amazon to keep up with supply and demand when it comes to pumping out millions of orders, usually in two days or less, while guaranteeing product accuracy and on time delivery.

How

An RV is your ticket to Camperforce. The program was designed for RVers looking for temporary employment while traveling in the United States. While campers come in all shapes and sizes, the bottom line is having one.

LAST WORDS

While the program is open to hiring applicants of all ages and physical strengths, it is wise not to overestimate your own capabilities.

These jobs are all very physical. Walking, standing for long periods, as well as lifting, bending and using multiple sets of stairs is required constantly throughout the day. Know your limits and make sure the job you sign up for is at a comfortable level within your physical ability.

CONTACT DETAILS

Web: amazondelivers.jobs/about/camperforce

Phone: 855-9CAMPER

Email: CamperForce@amazon.com

US ARMY CORP OF ENGINEERS

The United States Army Corp of Engineers (USACE) is responsible for almost 12 million acres of both land and water! It's a federal agency that maintains lakes, dams, marinas and campgrounds in various location in the US.

Not only does the Corp utilize volunteers and hire RVers, but it does so at more than 400 projects. They offer opportunities for outdoor hospitality at recreation resources through what they call the Volunteer Clearinghouse and Contract Bids.

VOLUNTEER POSITIONS

As you know donating your time in return for perks like onsite living, flexible hours and less strenuous work requirements is quite appealing to many people entering the Live Camp Work community, as well as those who desire a more laid-back approach.

Volunteering is also a great trial approach into workamping as it allows for many to gain valuable work experience, references, and even

launch several test trips prior to the actual commitment of diving in the deep end.

Although you are expected to serve without hourly pay, compensation for volunteer positions with USACE are often shorter in length, require less hours worked and come with a completely FREE site for the length of your agreed upon terms. As an added bonus, you actually receive the same benefits as federal employees since USACE is a federal employer- to my understanding.

WHAT CAN VOLUNTEERS DO?

At the Corps of Engineers, volunteers are utilized and needed in a variety of positions and roles. For those who appreciate natural settings and helping to maintain properties for public use, the Corps offers many positions in natural resource management as well as recreation.

While volunteering at the Corps, you may find more than one role where you are expected to help out and may fill in from time to time. As with many employers, hiring RVers that are willing to be helpful and pitch in is a high priority.

The number one volunteer position is the Park Host, as you can imagine. The positions are very popular in the RVing community and are highly sought after, making them pretty competitive.

As a Host, you may be required to provide helpful information to the general public, greet visitors, answer questions, register campers, take reservations, answer the phone, open and close the park gate, as well as collect camping and day use fees.

While camp hosting may be the most popular, the following positions are also great opportunities inside the Corps parks to consider:

9 Positions Inside the Park

1. Trail Maintenance
2. Visitor Center Staff
3. Education Program Staff
4. Park Facilities Staff
5. Landscaping & Maintenance
6. Onsite Tour Guides
7. Water Safety Program Presenter
8. Beach Clean Up
9. Habitat Restoration

HOW DO I APPLY?

If you are interested in volunteering with USACE, you'll have to get comfortable using the Volunteer Clearinghouse. This is a national information hub for all Corp projects which can be accessed either online at www.corpslakes.us/volunteer or by phone at -1-800-VOLUNTEER.

It's easy to apply and volunteer positions are always a great place to start for those who are new to workamping as well as those who have just never worked with the Corp.

From the Volunteer Clearinghouse you will be able to find information regarding the specific opportunities currently available as well as the contact information of the Volunteer Coordinator or Park Ranger who you will need to contact.

CONTRACT POSITIONS

Different from the volunteer positions, USACE also encourages relationships with independent contractors for some of the day-to-day operations inside the parks. These contracts are provided by individuals for specific jobs such as Park Attendant, Maintenance, Mowing, and in some instances can be provided as a larger group in what is called an 'umbrella contract'.

PARK ATTENDANT CONTRACTS

The Park Attendant is probably the most well-known, and possibly the most popular contract position with the Corp. In most situations, it will require 2 adults with no children under the age of 16, living onsite, providing the work needed to operate either a day use facility or campground.

The general agreement lasts between 4-7 months, usually in prime camping season, running from May-September and includes an RV site right by the entrance of the park. Working 8 hours per day for 5 days a week is a typical agreement. Evenings, weekends, holidays and even split shifts may be required.

Duties will vary by location and season, but most always include greeting visitors to the property and collecting fees.

Additional responsibilities can include maintaining a record of sites, using the NRRS reservation system, answering questions, surveillance, opening and closing the front gates, light housekeeping, and enforcing the listed quiet hours.

HOW TO PLACE BIDS

As a general rule, contracts will be awarded to the lowest qualified bidder.

If you've never bid on a government contract before, now is your chance to learn how! First things first, you'll need a copy of the contact specifications, that will list qualifications, deadlines, and procedures along with the bidding instructions.

Contacting the Park directly or the District Office will point you in the right direction for how to proceed. Make sure to ask to be placed on the mailing list to receive an invitation for bids.

The amount you bid is entirely up to you, but make sure you've at least decided on your bottom dollar hourly rate. Multiplying this number by the total amount of hours in the contract requirements should give you an idea of what you are looking at for the season.

Either use this number as your base figure, onto which you will add additional monies, or simply bid with this figure.

USACE is a great option for those who enjoy outdoor recreation and hospitality. They are also known for having some of the most beautiful campgrounds with great options for recreational opportunities. You will find many contacts in part 3 of this book, whom you can contact with your questions regarding specific projects and positions.

CALIFORNIA STATE PARKS

Sharing your time in exchange for rewards, such as the opportunity to live in some of the most beautiful and sought-after locations in California from beaches to mountains and just about everywhere in between, is one of the main benefits of volunteering in one of California's State Parks.

OVERVIEW

A vital part to overall success of California State Parks, volunteers make up a large part of the staff. You'll notice them working tirelessly to educate and teach the public about these valued locations scattered throughout the state. The system's properties include more than just your typical idea of a state park. It also includes a variety of treasured resources like historic monuments, lighthouses, historic homes, ghost towns, beaches, museums, visitor centers, and even off-road vehicle parks.

With over 40,000 volunteers to date who have contributed more than 1 million combined hours of dutiful

service, the California State Park system which according to the California Department of Parks and Recreation, now includes "280 state park units, over 340 miles of coastline, 970 miles of lake and river frontage, 15,000 campsites, and 4,500 miles of trails", continues to thrive and grow.

"Working for California State Parks is more than just a job, it's an opportunity to become a steward of some of the most important historic, beautiful and culturally significant resources in the state," said California State Parks Director Lisa Mangat in a recent press release. "Our employees work tirelessly to preserve delicate environments, modernize visitor connections through technology, and protect and uphold the law – all the while remaining dedicated to living the parks life throughout California."

Living the Parks Life is a phrase California State Parks uses to describe the life of those who work and volunteer inside the park system. They encourage people to "become a

California State Parks volunteer and BE the difference!".

WHY VOLUNTEER?

Many RVers are interested in volunteering for government agencies, charities and non-profits, where their hourly contribution is highly sought after. Their participation is heavily relied upon and the reward for such flows in forms other than monetary compensation.

Volunteering can be a very rewarding choice for RVers who desire experiences and benefits other than cash and have other means to sustain their travels such as savings, retirement or social security.

On the other hand, some folks have found that volunteering is an entrance ticket to paid positions or a way to gain experience in workamping when they are just starting out. These folks accept a volunteer gig in hopes of gaining experience and building their resume to give them a leg up for future positions down the road.

> *"Volunteering is just another way to work while you travel."*

It's a way to travel and see the country in exchange for work completed at various sites along the way.

I encourage you to think of the possibilities that working for an organization such as California State Parks would do, not only for you, but for the bigger goal of preserving and maintaining our country's natural resources.

As a volunteer you will have the opportunity to experience and learn history while living in a historical site and spending time in nature.

You can help maintain and preserve the state's natural environment and help habitats that are endangered or in need of repair. Many volunteers choose to take on these opportunities for the chance of making new friends, meeting new people and sharing the things they learn with the general public.

WHAT ARE SOME AVAILABLE POSITIONS?

There are many positions available for interested volunteers to choose from!

Your time and your skills will be contributing to maintaining the parks assets, visitor engagement, and sometimes behind the scenes tasks whose direct goals are to keep the parks operation up and running smoothly.

You can volunteer as a campground host and live onsite at one of many properties, or maybe help out in the visitor center and conduct tours as a docent. There are also opportunities available for roles in maintenance, safety patrol, and many others!

Docents:

A trained volunteer historian who interprets the natural and cultural features of the state parks. This is an amazing opportunity to have direct contact with park visitors. A highly trained position that requires continuous enrichment and training, Docents are able to receive the facts and information pertinent to the location and add their personal style into the delivery.

Job responsibilities may vary based on your location placement, but the opportunity to become involved with the educational programs, tours, living history reenactments and more, entice energetic folks to apply for these roles! People who are genuinely great with public speaking, have a knack for communications and a passion for sharing stories, are a great fit for these positions!

Public Safety Patrol:

The overall job of the Public Safety patrol volunteers is to provide safety information to the public. This includes; but is not limited to, first aid and emergency assistance that might be required during foot, boat, mountain bike, horseback or ATV patrol on property.

Park Hosts:

The most well-known job for a RVers is a Park Host. The Park Host is the face of the park.

A highly visible and accessible representative of the park system that assists day use and overnight visitors in a variety of ways from collecting fees, and cleaning facilities, to encouraging compliance with park rules and maybe even some light maintenance work.

The Park Host performs a broad range of job duties and is more like a jack of all trades than a master of one. These positions will usually require onsite living for ease of access and may require a 1-3-month commitment, or longer depending on the park. Some parks prefer long-term commitments, while other accept shorter stays from multiple hosts throughout the year.

In most cases the park host will work about 20-30 hours per week in exchange for their campsite, utilities and access to the facilities. While many parks offer full hookups, there are some parks who offer a more rustic experience and have partial hookups or none at all.

Visitor Center:

If you're best at customer service, then the Visitor Center might be the best place for your service inside the park system! Every business needs a smiling cheerful and moreover, helpful representative to greet visitors and provide accurate information! You can be that person as a Visitor Center Volunteer!

The main job duties will likely include answering questions in person and over the phone about the specific park amenities, trails, location and more, in addition to greeting guests onsite! Those who excel with direct contact with the public who also have great people skills and a friendly disposition should do well in these positions!

Natural Resource Protection:

These dedicated volunteers will play a critical role in the protection of natural resources in the California State Parks. Volunteers may be asked to assist with variety of hands-on jobs like exotic plant removal or relocations, trail maintenance and constructions, beach cleanups, habitat restorations and even native plant nurturing and enhancement projects.

With something always on the list to do, to add to the overall welfare of the park, the Natural Resource Protection volunteer is a great position for someone who likes to stay busy and work with nature!

SO HOW DO I APPLY?

My suggestion before applying for any position is to thoroughly research the park, the location, and to find out the amenities that will be offered in exchange for your time.

Since not all volunteer positions will likely come with the same benefits such as a campsite with full hookups, it's best to know up front what exactly you are applying for. Once you know for sure that the position is something you are interested in and capable of doing for the set time commitment, you'll want to complete a Volunteer in Parks Application.

Since each park is managed separately, you'll need to send your completed application to the volunteer coordinator at the park you are interested in working for. If applying to more than one location, be sure to send each location a separate copy of your application.

"On your application, put your best foot forward!"

These positions will be competitive, and the best applicant will end up getting the job. Take your time to fill out the application entirely and to your best ability, paying attention to the education and employment sections, as well as the background section and then attach a more detailed resume that further highlights your skills and experience!

Make sure to provide the information for three verifiable references who can vouch for your work ethic and abilities as they pertain to these positions. The more information you provide to the volunteer coordinator the better chances you'll have.

Volunteer opportunities are open to those over the age of 18. A medical and/or criminal background check may be required, along with a State Park Volunteer Application and a Volunteer Service Agreement.

Volunteers need to be both reliable and willing to complete assigned job duties, as like all RVer employers, the state parks rely on you to help them during their busiest times and efforts are said to be made to match your interests, skills and desires to the positions available.

CONTACT DETAILS

Web: www.livetheparkslife.com

Phone: (916) 653-9069

Email:
Volunteer.inparksprogram@parks.ca.gov

YELLOWSTONE NATIONAL PARK

If you're looking for an adventurous summer in the nation's oldest and most sought-after National Park, you'll be delighted to spend your time working for Delaware North at one of several General Stores & Hotels inside Yellowstone National Park!

Imagine what a few months spent exploring natural wonders like Old Faithful Geyser, would be like!

This could be the workamping adventure you've always dreamed of, and its more attainable than you might think! As a working RVer in Yellowstone, you will have the ultimate 'local' experience of living inside the park and the spectacular ability to go beyond what millions of tourists are able to see in short visits and really dig in!

DELAWARE NORTH

The National Park Service authorizes partners, such as Delaware North, to operate stores and hotels inside the park systems throughout the US. Delaware North operates about 300 stores in a variety of locations including Yellowstone, where 12 of its general stores are located along with three hotels in West Yellowstone.

As an employer, Delaware North does a great job to offer positions to a variety of people from all over the globe. From retirees to younger travelers, college students and everyone in-between, they hire a diverse group of people to help bring great experiences to visitors from all around the world!

WHY YELLOWSTONE?

When you make the decision to work at Yellowstone, you really make the decision to have a great summer! If you love the outdoors and/or have an urge to explore, this is the place for you!

"Yellowstone is the place to be for the summer, regardless of your age!"

This is the cream of the crop when it comes to workamping experiences because it offers so many activities for RVers to enjoy throughout their time there. So, as you can imagine there are many reasons why you would want to apply for a position to work at Yellowstone with Delaware North. Let's look at some of them.

5 Reasons to Choose Yellowstone:

1. Yellowstone is the world's first National park.
2. With 1,000 miles of hiking trails, everyone can find their perfect hike from day trips to backcountry excursions.
3. Home to more than 10,000 geysers, hot springs and fumaroles to explore at your leisure!
4. Employee Recreation Program Co-op: Offers trips around the park for employees like rafting, sporting events, talent shows, backpacking and more, all for FREE.
5. 30% Employee discounts, with select 50% off days throughout the season!

The Yellowstone workamping season usually starts early to mid-April and ends roughly at the end of November. Similar to Amazon Camperforce, you have the ability to provide a start date, and they will do their best to place you at one of their locations.

Expect to work 32-40 hours per week, per person. They hire singles, couples, and families, but make sure to discuss your scheduling needs up front.

Sometimes split shifts are required which might not work for families needing opposite shifts to account for childcare.

The team at Delaware North is very welcoming and do a great job of trying to accommodate everyone's needs. They also have a very straightforward approach to RV requirements… it just has to have all hard sides to be considered acceptable. Tents are not allowed.

COMPENSATION

I'll cut straight to the chase, working at Yellowstone will not make you rich! The wages are on the lower side of the average and start at about $9.50 (sometimes more) an hour, paid weekly. But before you count it out, because you need to take into consideration where you are able to live for a few months… for that reason, I approach working at Yellowstone as a job you take to explore the location, not one that pays for further travel adventures down the road.

Also, as a huge bonus, like literally, you will receive a $3 per hour bonus for all hours worked on your final paycheck when you complete the time agreement you signed up for!

That's a great bonus, when most employers offer $.50-$1.00 per hour bonuses!

LIVING AT YELLOWSTONE

Dormitories and RV sites are both available onsite living options for employees. RV campgrounds are shared with Xanterra employees but are not open to the public.

While FHU RV sites are not provided FREE with your employment, they are highly discounted and start at about $32 per week plus electric, which is payroll deductible. Most of the RV sites for staff are close to the stores, maybe a mile away, and if you are working at the Hotels, they are within walking distance.

Slides and size of the RV are some of the constraints of the available campgrounds.

Sites that accommodate long rigs and those with ample space for slides will be limited, so try to plan and apply early.

To my understanding, Yellowstone is considered to be very remote. Big box retailers, hospitals and general shopping are not close by and would require a trip to town to pick up necessary supplies and medications, or to be seen by a physician.

Optional Meal Plan

A dining meal plan is available for about $64.00 per week, but only for the staff working inside Yellowstone.

The meals are available 7 days a week and are payroll deductible, but you are only able to enroll and/or cancel this rotating menu one time during the season.

Workers with strict dietary needs, as well as those working at the West Yellowstone location, may have to make other plans for meals. The meal plan is optional, except for those staying in the dorms.

Employee Health Program

The seasonal staff health program known as Medcor, is not optional. Its required for all employees by the National Park Service and the cost is just under $8 per week.

Medcor isn't actual insurance or healthcare for that matter and should not be relied upon as such. It is more of a way to cover some of the costs of basic medical services offered at the three in park clinics, which are then offered at a discount to employees.

Limited Technology

It has been said that technology while living in Yellowstone is comparable to what was available more than a decade ago... this would obviously drive some folks crazy, while others will appreciate the chance to disconnect.

In some parts of the park the internet and cell phone connectivity are limited, and in others it's totally unavailable. Be prepared for this experience and think carefully on how being limited in your connectivity will affect you. Wi-Fi is available, though very limited, and some dorms have computers with internet available.

Verizon is the best cell provider in the park and pay phones are available at all locations.

Receiving Your Mail

Most of the locations have a seasonal post office for you to receive packages and mail. You can have your mail forwarded to these locations, but keep in mind, you will be unable to forward it back- so it's suggested you stop the forwarding 2-3 weeks before your end date.

AVAILABLE POSITIONS

Most, if not all positions, are physically demanding and can be quite strenuous at altitudes between 6,000-8,000 feet.

- Inside the General Stores
- Cashier/Retail Assistant
- Cash Room Associate
- Stocker
- Warehouse Associate
- Employee Dining Room Cook
- Grill Cook
- Kitchen Assistant
- Custodian
- Inside the West Yellowstone Hotels
- Front Desk Clerk
- Host/Cashier
- Retail Clerk
- Housekeeper
- Laundry Attendant
- Line Cook
- Server/Bartender

CONTACT DETAILS

Website: www.ygsjobs.com

Phone: 406-586-7593

Email: ygsjobs@delawarenorth.com

AGS PUBLICATIONS

Earn extra income as you travel with AGS Publications as part of their driving sales team for the campground industry.

As one of the industry leaders in providing guest guides, campground maps, along with an array of digital marketing and web design services for campgrounds and RV resorts, AGS Publications has been in business for over 30 years since it was first founded in 1986.

WHY AGS?

AGS hires full-time RVers to join their team as Sales Representatives to sell advertising for guest guides that parks and campgrounds will then hand out to their guests upon arrival.

If you've seen a guide in person, then you already know they are high-quality colored campground maps that also include pertinent traveler information like park rules, internet channels, dog walk locations, as well as a variety of local business options that travelers may find of interest.

By representing a wide variety of privately owned campgrounds, RV resorts, as well as popular camping brands like KOA, Thousand Trails, Encore Resorts, and Jellystones, the Sales Representatives at AGS Publications have the ability to crisscross the map from east to west and north to south as they travel and earn big commissions along the way!

Joining the ranks of the AGS Sales Representative Team allows you to define your travels from the very start. Unlike some other companies where leads are required, at AGS you are not alone in setting up your assignments. In fact, their home office handles this for you, so you don't have to search for new assignments.

Since you will typically only be working in 2-week increments, you can travel as much as you want, while bringing in a great income to boot.

On your way from one assignment to the next, you can enjoy the freedom to stop and sightsee all the many things you've dreamed about when entering the RV lifestyle.

ABOUT THE JOB

Corporate training is provided to help ensure you are equipped with the knowledge you need to be successful and the tools you need to get the job done. Your training will last between 5-7 days and will be conducted by a corporate trainer, who is also a working representative.

After successful completion, you will be given a number of assignments to begin immediately along with the confidence you need to hit the streets running.

Since your main job is to sell advertising to the local businesses surrounding the campgrounds and RV parks, you have the awesome benefit of staying in the park for 2 weeks, free of charge, while you scour the streets for sales!

You will need to know your market of fellow RVers and be able to identify the local businesses that will most likely benefit from advertising to RVers. These businesses might be RV specific or just traditional products and services they could find useful during their stay in the area.

The guest guides are provided to the business at no cost and are actually paid for through your advertising sales, which I would think makes for an easy sell!

You are only required to work 12-15 jobs per year but can request for additional assignments to make extra income if desired. Commissions are reported to reach as high as 70% of ads sold and are easily direct deposited into your bank account. You'll be happy to know they start from the very first sale! This is one job for RVers that allows for great income along with short stays and great travel opportunities!

JOB REQUIREMENTS

This is my own personal opinion, but I do believe you need a knack for sales, a generally friendly disposition and the ability to talk to people in depth about the benefits of purchasing these products to be successful. Sales are not for everyone, but for those who grasp how to do it and do it well, the opportunities are endless, and the income can be huge!

AGS starts with an application that you can find on their website and then progresses applicants through a three-stage interview process.

This method has allowed them to lead the pack with the lowest turnover in the industry by completing a full exchange of information and ideas. Their ultimate goal is to make sure there are no hidden surprises on either side once they bring in a new Sale Representative to join their growing team.

AGS Publications typically looks for applicants that meet the following criteria:

- Full-time RVers, with at least 6 months experience or several years of prior RVing.
- One team member needs a sales background.
- Willingness to work at least 12-15 two-week assignments per year.
- Must remain in contact with the office whenever an assignment is in production.
- Basic computer skills including email.
- Must be willing to attend the annual meeting every March to learn about new products & services.
- Flexible travels, as you must be open to go where the jobs are available.
- Must be driven and professional!

CONTACT DETAILS

Website:
https://www.agspub.com/rep-team-information/

Phone: 1-877-518-1989

Email: info@agspub.com

ADVENTURELAND PARK

If you are looking to spend the summer some place where fun is plentiful, consider working at Adventureland Amusement Park.

In addition to the amusement park, Adventureland includes 200+ acres that also houses a 310-site campground and an almost 200 room hotel, just East of Des Moines in Altoona, IA right off exit I-80. A popular summer hangout, more than 600,000 guests are expected for the 2018 season!

Since Des Moines is just a short drive away, there is much to see and do in your leisure time while working inside the park. RVers should consider using days off to visit place like the Botanical Center, Farmer's Markets, Blank Park Zoo, the State Capital, the Science Center and many other top attractions like the State Capital.

WORKING AT ADVENTURELAND

The Adventureland workamping program, which dates back many years of successfully hiring RVers, has become a very well-known summer job.

Over the years, RVers have returned to work for Adventureland year after year and many have brought friends and family back to join the fun experience. Throughout the season, they do a good job of encouraging employees to have a good time as well. It is reported that trips to local attractions, group games, ice cream socials, and other social activities are planned for employees to interact and have some summer fun.

Compensation includes a free FHU campsite during the season provided each RVer is available to work up to 40 hours a week. Pay is calculated for all hours worked and starts around $8.50 per hour.

Separate from other workamping programs, they do not set time constraints on when your work agreement ends but do offer a seasonal bonus for those who stay through the end of the operational season. The end of season bonus is calculated at $.75 for every hour worked and an additional $400 campsite bonus is possible, if the majority of the occupants of a campsite are working during the season.

The HR Director has been known to start hiring right after Labor Day for the next season, but typically likes to wait until October 1.

While the workamping season at Adventureland runs from late April to late September, they seem to have flexible start dates with the caveat that all RVers should be onsite by late June.

In April, at the beginning of the season, schedules will include part-time weekend hours only.

Once the park opens for the summer and operations are in full swing, RVers can expect to see daily full-time hours through the last weekend in September where 8 hours days, 5-6 days per week are normal.

POSITIONS AVAILABLE

Most positions will be inside the park facility in departments such as ride operations, retail, food service, and retail working 5-7 hour days with a 30-minute unpaid break.

Rides

Working in the rides department will include operating amusement park rides for park guests. Primary duties include assisting guests during the loading and unloading process and guest safety is a top priority.

Standing on your feet for extended periods of time is typical in these roles, and they also require moderate lifting. You will be exposed to various weather conditions, so make sure you have appropriate gear.

Food Service

Food service employees are required to take and fill orders, operate the cash register, accept cash payments, and prepare some food items.

Standing on your feet for extended periods of time is typical in these roles, and they also require moderate lifting when receiving and unpacking inventory. Safety is a top priority and requirements include use of (PPE) personal protective equipment.

Games

Inside the games department, RVers can expect to work in many arcade and game areas throughout the park.

Major responsibilities will include encouraging players to play games, handling cash payments, providing prizes to winners, and speaking over a microphone. Basic customer service and math skills are needed, along with an outgoing personality due to high guest interaction.

Folks working in this department can expect to be exposed to various weather elements.

Retail

Retail Employees will enjoy working in one of several kiosks and/or souvenir shops throughout the park. Locations are located both indoors and outdoors, with varying weather elements. Job responsibilities might include tasks such as, using a register with point of sale computer, credit card processing, and stocking shelves.

Employees in these roles should enjoy high customer interactions and be ready for a really fast-paced work environment.

DRESS CODE

Adventureland has a dress code that is required for all employees.

They will provide two work shirts, a sweatshirt and a raincoat. A $15 uniform deposit will be withheld from your first paycheck until the items are returned.

You are responsible for providing:

- Low cut black or white sneakers.
- A black belt, if wearing black shoes.
- A brown belt, if wearing white shoes.
- Khaki shorts, pants or capris.

CONTACT DETAILS

Web: adventurelandresort.com/employment/workamper

Phone: 1-800-532-1286

Email: hr@adventurelandpark.com

BOWLIN TRAVEL CENTERS

Workamping opportunities inside the Bowlin Travel Center family means working at one of ten travel centers, five Dairy Queens, or Subway locations in Arizona and New Mexico.

Open 365 days a year, boasting long operating hours like 7am - 7pm, Bowlin is not your typical workamping job. In fact, for some folks it's a workamping career- that allows you to live onsite.

WORKING AT BOWLIN

Working at Bowlin includes customer service and sales.

You will be working in a location that sells a combination of retail items, specialty gifts, gas, and food. These positions do not require experience beyond your typical customer service capabilities. The positions are hands on and require individuals who are self-motivated and enjoy public interaction.

Positions also require a variety of job responsibilities that include the willingness to do everything from cleaning restrooms to daily paperwork.

Doing whatever it takes to deliver a great customer experience is a top priority.

Bowlin employees usually work a 40-hour week. Hourly wages are paid in addition to a 5% commission for sales over a set threshold of about $50. While at work, Bowlin requires that employees cover all visible tattoos and that all piercings beyond one in each ear (for women only) be removed.

POSITIONS

A variety of positions are available inside the Bowlin brand depending on the location. Each location is different, and some will not offer all positions or possibly the same pay. Make a note to ask about availability at all open locations to make sure you are looking at the most attractive positions for that time.

Full Time & Part Time Positions Include:

- Manager-In-Training in Travel Center
- Manager-In-Training in Dairy Queen
- Customer Service/Sales
- Retail Clerks
- Maintenance/Custodial
- Inventory Specialist

LOCATIONS

All locations are located in either New Mexico or Arizona.

Some are closer to the surrounding towns than others, and some can be downright remote.

I-10

- Akela Flats Travel Center
- Butterfield Stations & Dairy Queen
- Continental Divide Travel Center
- Old West Trading Post
- Picacho Peak Travel Center & Dairy Queen
- The Thing Travel Center & Dairy Queen

I-40

- Bluewater Outpost & Dairy Queen
- Flying C Ranch & Dairy Queen

US 70

- Running Indian at Alamogordo

BENEFITS

One of the best parts about working for Bowlin are the employee benefits.

Unlike other workamping employers, Bowlin offers a great compensation plan including pay for all hours worked, additional commission payouts, FREE on-site RV parking, 401k plan, paid vacations days, sick leave, bereavement and personal days, dental, vision and life insurance as well as uniform shirts and employee discounts!

CONTACT DETAILS

Web: www.bowlintc.com

Phone: 888-240-7746

Email: humanresources@bowlintc.com

KAMPGROUNDS OF AMERICA

Kampgrounds of America, known as KOA to campers and travelers alike, has a unique workamping program that stems from the ownership of more than 500 campgrounds throughout the United States.

KOA developed its RV jobs with one extra special benefit... the ability to acquire travel vouchers for comped stays at KOA properties on your way to your next assignment!

WORKAMPING AT KOA

Hiring seasonal employees for predetermined time periods, KOA brings RVers both retired and non, into their parks to help supplement their income while traveling in North America. Recently, KOA has seen a more diverse variety like many other RV employers of families with children and folks who are much younger than traditional RVers coming into their workamping program.

RVers are hired for a variety of job roles and commitment times, ranging from part-time and seasonal to full-time and year long. Most RVers will be hired for about 6 months during the peak travel season depending on location and the park that you are interested in working at.

Each campground will indicate how many hires they will need for any given time. Each park will also decide what the compensation will be for each position, although benefits like health insurance are never provided.

TYPICAL JOBS

Based on the campground you are interested in working at, you'll have the opportunity to apply for a variety of typical campground positions ranging from Recreation Directors and Reservations, to Housekeeping and Maintenance.

If you are open to traveling to different areas of the country and keep an open mind on what positions are available during the season you are applying for, I would think finding a position with KOA would be towards the easy side of the spectrum. If it's a numbers game, which I believe it always is, then having the added bonus of applying for a position with a company with hundreds of site opportunities would lead one to believe the odds are in your favor.

POSITIONS AT KOA

- Park Management
- Front Desk Clerk/Retail
- Reservations/Office Staff
- Campground Host
- Activity Director
- Recreations Staff
- Site Escort
- Housekeeping
- Grounds Crew
- Landscaping
- Maintenance

LIVING ON-SITE

Although on-site living is sometimes required with the KOA RV jobs program, almost all the KOA properties will require you to make arrangements for your own housing.

This can either be living on-site in your own RV, living off-site in traditional housing, or living on-site in housing provided by the property. (If provided housing is something you are interested in, you will have the added responsibility of contacting the specific park and inquiring about the availability with them directly.)

MEMBERSHIP REQUIRED

Finding the jobs at KOA is a little different than finding your traditional workamping jobs as they keep the majority of their posting on an internal membership site. To access the sites listings and information, you will have to purchase a yearly membership that costs about $35.

It should be noted that many parks still advertise their positions on FREE job boards like WorkampingJobs.com and CoolWorks.com

What's Included In The Membership?

- Access to KOA job postings
- Ability to post KOA resume
- *On the Road* e-newsletter for KOA Work Kampers
- Eligible for KOA Work Kamper of the Year award
- Travel vouchers to get from one job to the next!
- Referral rewards for recruiting friends
- KOA workamping gift after finishing your first job.

CONTACT

Web: www.workatkoa.com

Email: welovekamping@koa.net

SOUTHERN CROSS

Southern Cross is an RV employer who hires 'mobile leak survey technicians' that they kindly refer to as 'travelers' whose main job responsibility is to inspect gas lines to make sure they are working properly and then report the findings.

Natural gas lines have to be inspected regularly, that means every 5 years in most cases, but also every year for hospitals, schools, and business areas. As you can imagine, there is no shortage of work when it comes to identifying and ultimately preventing catastrophic situations. Most of the time the gas lines are said to be working as they should, but in the event where an issue is detected, your findings would be reported to the utility provider.

One assignment might have you assigned to a busy commercial district inside a metro area while the next would take you deep into a rural community where daily interaction with farm animals would not be uncommon.

Talk about variety- RVers who are always up for new adventures and don't mind less than adventurous jobs to get them there will do just great in these positions.

OVERVIEW

A position with Southern Cross is not your typical workamping job where you are on assignment for a specific amount of time then move on to another employer.

In fact, it could be considered a mix of the best of both worlds since you work for one employer while traveling to new destinations with each new assignment.

Both singles and couples are welcome to apply, but the one stipulation you should be aware of is that each person is treated like an individual employee. While couples would be placed on the same projects, transportation to work might get tricky trying to coordinate jobs in and around different areas.

And since they offer year-round employment, an RVer looking for a more permanent or reliable position without the need to line up gigs as they go, but still enjoy traveling to new cities both large and small might see this type of employment offer as a viable choice.

At Southern Cross you would be given one job assignment at a time, for a specific amount of time, then move on to your next assignment in a new location without gaps in employment or benefits.

"each project is different"

Some last from just a few weeks in small towns or rural areas, while others might extend for months in larger metropolitan areas.

Assignments are said to never exceed 11 months. To my understanding, you would know up front what the time on each assignment would be as you are scheduled. T

hey also make an effort to try to schedule travelers to an assignment for at least a month, so that you can negotiate a lower rental rate with the local campgrounds, which is an extra effort in my opinion to accommodate RVers and just a kind gesture on behalf of the employer.

TYPICAL DAY

Working for Southern Cross means working the hours of their clients on each project. That usually means 7am-3:30pm.

In a perfect world, you would leave your RV campground in the morning and arrive at your assigned location at the designated time. Working at your own pace, you would walk over the buried gas lines (which are either under the sidewalks or slightly to the side) using your handheld instrument to 'sniff' the area for methane and check gas meters.

Entering yards is typical to access the gas meters, which might require you to contact the homeowner to gain access if blocked or enclosed. Navigating according to the provided map, your day would continue until your day is complete and you return to your RV for the night.

COMPENSATION

Personally, I think Southern Cross has one of the best compensation packages for RVers.

They hire employees, not independent contractors which means each traveler will have applicable taxes withheld from their hourly wages and they also offer benefits including health insurance, paid time off, paid holidays and 401K enrollment, which are hard to find from workamping employers.

As if that wasn't enough, they also provide some really great perks for their employees which include covering some common living and travel related expenses, including mileage reimbursement and a per diem which are both not taxed.

Popular Benefits

- Starting hourly rate at $11.00/hr.
- $300.00 Per diem per week. (RV site and living expenses)
- Daily vehicle mileage is reimbursed at the IRS rate.
- RV reassignment mileage is reimbursed (when moving the RV from one project to the next). This reimbursement rate is .25 cents above the current IRS rate.

An end of project bonus is occasionally provided but should not be factored into anticipated earnings.

A FEW THINGS TO KNOW

- Survey technicians work outdoors in all weather conditions.
- They must be physically fit and able to walk 6-8 miles per day

on varied terrain 8 hours per day, 5 days per week.
- Also requires the ability to be able to repeatedly lift their arms over their heads. Our first priority is the safety of our team, so we promote a culture of taking our time and staying safe.
- A large portion of the job is actually documenting our work on I-Pads, Android tablets and PC based laptops. Therefore, the ability to interact with technology is required.
- Map reading skills are a plus.
- Each technician must have viable transportation. This could be the tow vehicle (pick-up) or small car towed behind a motorhome.
- Every technician must have a valid driver's license and vehicle insurance.
- Travelers must find and secure their own RV park.

CONTACT INFORMATION

Web: www.southerncrossinc.com

Phone: 800-241-5057

Email: info@southerncrossinc.com

ALASKA EXCURSIONS

What embodies the working RVer lifestyle more than great jobs in great places?

A cool job in an awesome place, that's what! And if you're looking into jobs that will provide adventures not only along the way, but also through your days, consider Alaska Excursions for a workamping adventure to remember!

ABOUT ALASKA X

Alaska Excursions, or AlaskaX, is a newbie in the RVing community.

Their quickly growing tour company offers a wide variety of positions for RVers looking to join their team in Skagway, Alaska for the summer. Skagway is a well-known, small town in southeast Alaska.

Mild temperatures during the prime summer season make it an ultra-desirable location for outdoor enthusiasts and travelers alike. Hiking trails, gorgeous scenery and a variety of wildlife make taking a trip to Alaska for the summer an extra special bucket list item for many RVers!

COMPENSATION:

As part of the AlaskaX team, you will be paid for all hours worked at an hourly rate of $12-$15 depending on your position. As an additional benefit, you will have the ability to experience all of their offered public tours for free as well as the ability to take advantage of other local tours for free or at a reduced rate.

Employee housing is available for staff members to rent in the town of Skagway.

There is a free employee shuttle for those working outside the city with picks ups both to and from work locations. For those driving up in their RVs, AlaskaX has a private RV park located in town as well! Sites include water/sewer/electric and are available for $550 per month.

A typical season runs from the end of April to the end of September.

If you can make the commitment to stay for the whole season, your application will be given preference over a partial season applicant, so keep that in mind when applying, just don't overextend yourself where you might have a problem completing your whole assignment.

They do offer an end of the season bonus for employees based on completion of the season and a performance review. Staff members who complete their employment agreements and receive a positive review are eligible to earn a full bonus calculated at $2 per hour for each hour worked.

WORKING FOR ALASKAX

A typical day at AlaskaX is face paced with a lot of guest interaction! You can expect days lasting 8 hours on average in many positions and up to 9-11 for others. Your start and end times will vary by position, but in general will not be before 6:30am or after 8:00 pm.

Overnights are also not a concern. Staffers can expect to work 4-5 days each week, leaving you some time to get out and explore the beautiful area and create some Alaska memories to take with you after the season!

Hiring both singles and couples, AlaskaX evaluates each applicant on an individual basis for the position they have applied. They do make an effort to accommodate both couples and friends with scheduling requests as often as possible. If you want same days off or opposite days off, you will need to bring this scheduling concern to their attention early on in the hiring process.

POPULAR POSITIONS

Providing the best possible guest experience with the greatest tour and excursions possible is one of their main goals, so being exceptional in customer services as well as a team player will be vital skills! Keep in mind that while they do accept applications for all positions and are happy to train the right individual, preference is given to applicants who have prior experience in the area they are applying.

Also, AlaskaX utilizes Skype interviews so they can meet potential hires during the application process. These will be scheduled after your application is reviewed.

Adventure Guide:

Adventure Guides are tasked with the job of guiding guests on an adventure they will remember forever. Warmly greeting guests while safely driving and providing them with an entertaining tour along the way is a top priority.

Guides usually stay with the guests all throughout the excursion entertaining them along the way and completing other tasks like picking up litter, cleaning guest bathrooms, and keeping the refreshment area stocked.

Office & Dock Staff:

Provide guests with their first impression either over the phone, through an email, or in person. The company's first point of contact for ship staff and other local companies, you will make sure all of the ships leave on time with the correct number of people on board.

Making snacks and drinks for the different tours, selling tickets to prospective guests, handling guest reservations are all in a day's work!

This position is great for people who thrive in really fast-paced working environments, enjoy engaging with people and are always up for a new challenge.

Groundskeeper:

If you have a green thumb and a love of the outdoors, this position might be right for you! Your days will be spent brightening buildings with flowers and lush lawns, maintaining workspaces and natural trails.

To excel in these positions, AlaskaX suggests staffers be physically fit and able to complete days of physically demanding repetitive motions and extensive walking in all types of weather.

Photographer:

Help capture guest excitement and experiences as part of the photography staff. Take pictures during excursions that are then provided for sale in the gift shop. Capturing the excitement of the moment is your main responsibility and being able to use creativity to precise timing will serve you well in these positions.

This position is fast-paced and requires the skill to position photos for all types of weather.

Retail Sales Associate:

Assisting store customers in onsite gift shops also includes working in the coffee shop/bar and the photo sales department.

Welcoming new guests, answering questions, offering assistance, and handling cash/credit cards at the register are all daily tasks in this position.

Maintenance:

The maintenance staff performs a wide range of tasks throughout the company. These include, but are not limited to repairing, servicing, and building equipment of various sorts. They operate equipment such as loaders, excavators, dump trucks, and work vehicles.

They even do things such as cut trees as well as build fences and cabins. They perform any task that is needed throughout the company.

HIRING PROCESS

- Submit an online application.
- They will contact you for more information and to discuss details to move forward.
- Skype interview is scheduled.
- Employment decision generally made within a week.

CONTACT DETAILS

Web: www.alaskaexcursions.com/employment

Email: Jobs@AlaskaX.com

Phone: (907) 209-606

MICHIGAN LIGHTHOUSE KEEPERS

The job of a Lighthouse Keeper is anything but your typical 9-5 office job.

In fact, it's not your typical job by any means and was actually one of the hardest jobs just 100 years ago, with the need to spend extended periods on a small parcel of land usually in the middle of the water, with sailors' lives depending on your reliability and faithful attention to keeping the light lit.

Working 24-hour shifts, 7 days a week was the typical schedule and allowed for each Keeper to light the tower's lamp each night before dusk and make sure it stayed lit until the sun came up the next morning.

In addition, their jobs required them to take care of the whole lighthouse station and that meant preforming many jobs while making sure sailors had safe passage.

COMMON JOB DUTIES

- Light the lamp at sunset and keep it burning until sunrise.
- Sweep the floors.
- Clean tower windows
- Paint, clean and do minor repair work
- Maintain equipment
- Maintain Keeper logbook
- Take weather readings daily
- Weed the walkways.
- Maintain the grounds.
- Lend assistance to ships and sailors in distress
- Keep inventory of lighthouse equipment and fuel.
- Maintain light station boat launch.
- Keep boathouse clean
- Provide visitors with tour of light station as needed.

"But The Days Of These Types Of Lighthouse Keeper Jobs Are Long Gone."

Today many states have lighthouses that offer a Keeper program run by non-profits whose main goal is to preserve their history. These programs are run in different ways but the overall general theme seems to be Keeper for a fee or donation or membership, meaning you'll pay a relatively small fee to participate in the program.

Members of the public are invited to volunteer at historic lighthouses for short terms of a few days to several weeks, as supporting members of the non-profits that operate them. Fees can range from less than $50 to over $100, but each provides the operating organization with valuable funds to fuel the day to day costs of keeping these pieces of history alive and open to the public!

In this chapter I'd like to feature several of the Lighthouse Keeper programs I found in midwestern state of Michigan which borders four of the five Great Lakes!

MICHIGAN LIGHTHOUSES

Have you ever imagined what it would be like to spend a few weeks on an island as a lighthouse keeper?

Imagine the serenity of being totally isolated in the middle of the water, with just you, your spouse, a good friend or maybe your family.

And while not all lighthouses are technically on islands miles off the coast, taking a few weeks to work at one of Michigan's beautiful historic lighthouses this year could be an amazing journey for an adventurous Work Camper couple, single or family who wants to switch things up with a job that's far from being a traditional camp host and will supply a lifetime of campfire stories to share at will.

Michigan has one of our nation's most active waterways with over 3200 miles of coastlines. So, it's really no surprise that they would have the most lighthouses out of all 50 states, which are still used as waypoints and landmarks for sailors, history buffs and tourists alike.

Most of Michigan's lighthouses are owned by organizations or private citizens who have turned them into a bed and breakfasts, museums or conduct seasonal tours.

The few Lighthouse Keeper programs that still exists are definitely worth looking into for job openings but be forewarned that each one is run completely separate and are designed individually.

LIGHTHOUSE PROGRAMS WITH RV CAMPING

Lighthouse keeper programs are few and far between but finding one with RV camping on property is like finding a needle in a haystack!

Programs like the one offered at Forty Mile Point Lighthouse and Crisp Lighthouse allows for Keepers to use their own RV's as on-site living quarters, which provide all the comforts of home.

FORTY MILE POINT, ROGERS CITY

Located inside the Presque Isle County's Lighthouse Park, Forty Mile Point Lighthouse actually includes the lighthouse museum, gift shop and Calcite Pilot House which are open to the public from Memorial Day Weekend to Mid-October each year. Normal operating hours are from Tuesday – Saturday 10 am to 4 pm or Noon to 4 pm on Sundays. The lighthouse is operated by the 40 Mile Point Lighthouse Society which is dedicated to its restoration and preservation.

This program hosts 4 Lighthouse Keepers at all times, and they request all Keepers commit to a minimum stay of 2 weeks.

During your stay, Keepers are usually allowed to coordinate the schedule by themselves to make sure all hours are covered, and each Keeper has one day off per week, in addition to Monday when the property is closed. It's not uncommon to have groups of school children, adult organizations and clubs, reunion parties, as well as birthday and wedding celebrations on-site, so unlike other lighthouse properties, this particular program is well used and visited.

All Light Keepers are required to supply their own RVs for on-site RV camping during their commitments at Forty Mile Point.

There are four fully self-contained RV camping spots onsite for Keepers use, which are located south of the on-site pavilion. Two RV spaces are reserved for current Keepers and two are reserved for the incoming Keepers, which allows for a smooth transition. Tents are not allowed on property.

Main Duties

- Welcoming visitors.
- Learn and provide historical information about the museum.
- Operating and managing the gift shop, light house museum and the pilot house.
- Sweeping floors, sidewalks and tower stairs as needed.
- Stock items in the gift shop and keep it well maintained.
- Light cleaning duties including dusting, vacuuming and trash removal.
- Public Speaking.
- Operate cash register and credit card machine.

- Activate and de-activate the security system daily.

Things To Know

- Small pets are allowed on-site, as long as they are on a 6ft leash.
- Food and beverages are not allowed in the gift shop.
- Excessive alcohol consumption is not allowed.
- Campfires are only allowed in the provided fire rings.

Contact Info

Web: http://www.40milepointlighthouse.org/assist.html

Phone: (989) 372-6090
Email: lhpark@gmx.com

CRISP POINT LIGHTHOUSE

In 1876, Crisp Point Lighthouse was one of just four Lifesaving stations set up for service along the "Shipwreck Coast" of Lake Superior.

Formerly known as Station #10, it soon took the name of Cristopher Crisp, its second keeper who served from 1878-1890. After almost being completely lost to history, Don & Nellie Ross formed the Crisp Point Light Historical Society in an effort to preserve the main tower. Today Crisp Point Lighthouse is operated by the Crisp Point Light Historical Society (CPLHS), a non-profit organization whose mission is to restore and preserve the lighthouse for future generations!

Operating a Lighthouse Keeper program to keep the facility staffed for visitor access to the tower and the visitor center, CPLHS seeks volunteers to donate 8 hours of their time, daily, for 1-5 days spans. Daily operation at this lighthouse is said to have busy days with a variety of guests and peaceful nights that provide fantastic stargazing!

The typical schedule is 10am-6pm with the ability to host groups of 2-4 Keepers at a time, who are welcome to have children, although they do not count as Keepers and use the primitive camping spot onsite for their RV.

Main Duties

- Open the tower and Visitor Center for guests to access.
- Greet visitors, sell Crisp Point related merchandise and answer questions.
- Provide information about the lighthouse and the Historical Society.
- Pick up debris and other items found on the grounds.
- Sweep and clean lighthouse and Visitor Center building as needed.
- Clean and restock restrooms as needed.
- Sweep boardwalk as needed.

• Restock merchandise containers with extra stock.

Things To Know

• You are not required to stay at the lighthouse to volunteer as a Keeper. In town lodging and camping options are close by.
• There is a cement pad near the visitor center, where RVs that are self-contained can park for the duration of their stay.
• Drinking water is not available onsite. Prepare to bring your own!
• Electricity is not available for personal use. Prepare to bring a generator.
• Trashcans/dumpster are not available onsite.
• A landline is available for use at the visitor center.
• Buildings are not heated.
• Pets are welcome but need to be leashed.
• BBQ grill and campfire pit are available onsite.

Crisp Point accepts applications for prospective keepers on a first come first serve basis, starting each year in November, but are currently still looking for a few dates for 2019!

To apply for the Keeper program, you must purchase a membership with CPLHS, which are $20-30 per year, and contact Jamie Rolfe with the Historical Society, to schedule your time on the Keeper schedule.

Contact Info

Web: http://www.crisppointlighthouse.org

Phone: Jamie Rolfe 616-204-1729
Email: cplhs1944@gmail.com

LIGHT KEEPER PROGRAMS WITH ON-SITE HOUSING

Regardless of if you have an RV or not, working at a lighthouse might still be something adventurous you want to experience.

If this sounds like you, then the following Lighthouse Keeper Programs are more typical than those that have onsite camping options. These programs provide on-site housing for the Keeper's use during their commitment.

Accommodations will vary with each property, but you can expect at the very least to have a basic indoor sleeping area. Some properties will boast full refurbished units with bunk beds, sleeper sofa for guests, fresh paint and indoor plumbing.

SOUTH FOX ISLAND LIGHT STATION

South Fox Light Station is 20 miles offshore in the middle of Lake Michigan.

Funds were first appropriated for its construction on March 2, 1876 in an effort to provide sailors with the ability to make night crossing and protect anchorage in the shadow of the island.

Sitting at the southern tip of the property, which also includes privately owned acres, the South Fox Light Station contains 115 acres and houses 7 original structures.

The station is maintained by the Fox Island Lighthouse Association (FILA), which is a volunteer non-profit group that is dedicated to the preservation of the Light Station through community involvement.

Working in partnership with the Michigan Department of Natural Resources, FILA strives to maintain historical accuracy and welcomes volunteer Lighthouse Keepers during the summer months.

Commitments of 2, 3, or 4 weeks can help keep buildings open to the public and provide tours for visitors.

Living as a Keeper on South Fox Island means spending 2-4 weeks on an remote island where you have the option to sleep inside the Keepers living quarters or pitch a tent on a beautiful island and enjoy the great outdoors!

It also means keeping busy with work that could always be done. From being docents to occasional visitors, to performing ground maintenance, painting, beach grooming and much more- there is always something for Keepers to do.

This position is well suited for those who like to be left to enjoy beautiful areas, without daily chit chat with neighbors, luxuries like refrigeration, running water, and flush toilets.

Main Duties

• Keep watch light station and other buildings.
• Complete small projects like painting and light carpentry.
• Maintain property landscape by cutting grass and clearing brush.
• Open buildings for tours visitors who will arrive by water.
• Cots in rooms available for up to 6 or you can bring a tent. This is a volunteer position there is no pay.

Things To Know

• You are required to live on-site during your whole commitment.
• The position requires the ability to climb stairs.

- This is an isolated off-grid location.
- There is no electric on site.
- There is no drinking water on the island. Bring a water filter or bottles.
- Solar is available to charge phones.
- A generator is provided for use with tools.
- Water transportation is available to and from the island by FILA
- FILA requires a $200 deposit to hold your position. It is refundable upon arrival.

If you're interested in volunteering at the South Fox Light Station, please note there are many great RV parks in Leelanau County, where you could easily stay for a few weeks or a month and explore the area in between weeks.

Contact Info

Web: www.southfox.org

Catherine Allchin: 231-883-7645 or miboatlady@gmail.com
Phil Von Voigtlander: 231-640-0054 or Philfvon@gmail.com

TAWAS POINT LIGHTHOUSE

Formerly known as Ottawa Point after Chief O-ta-was, who was the leader of the Saginaw band of Chippewas, Tawas Point Lighthouse stood forty-five feet tall with a six-foot base at construction back in 1850! The first Keeper, Sherman Wheeler lived in a 5-room brick dwelling on-site and was paid about $350 as an annual salary.

Located inside the Tawas Point State Park, Tawas Point Lighthouse attracts visitors from around the world, with two historic shipwrecks sitting right off the shoreline! With ample opportunities for hiking, birdwatching, and ideal conditions for swimming- Tawas Point is a popular point of interest for travelers from May- October each year.

The Lighthouse Keepers Program is operated by the Michigan History Center (MHC) which provides volunteers with a unique opportunity to live onsite, while helping to preserve and present its history of one of Michigan's most notable lighthouses to the public. Keepers serve in teams of two to four people at a time, which can be a combination of friends and/or family, and the program runs from May 1 through October 29 each year.

This program provides on-site housing in a second story Keeper's quarters that are provided for your use during your stay. Two bedrooms, with sleeping for up to four adults along with a full kitchen, bathroom and free parking is provided.

Main Duties

- Provide tours to the public Thursday- Monday, at scheduled times.

• Must be comfortable with public speaking.
• Greet visitors in a friendly manner.
• Provide information about the lighthouse and the surrounding area.
• Basic facility maintenance.
• Trash removal and routine cleaning tasks.
• Maintaining outside walkways and windows.

Things To Know

• Must be able to serve a full 2-week term.
• A $75 per person fee is required.
• Keepers must be 18 years or older.
• Pets are not allowed.
• Keepers must be willing to provide tours five days a week.
• Typical schedule is about 35 hours per week.
• A background check is required.
• Keepers must be able to climb the 85-step lighthouse tower.

Contact Information

Website: www.michigan.gov/tawaslighthouse

Email: dnr-tawaskeepers@michigan.gov

Phone: 989-348-2537

SABLE POINTS LIGHTHOUSE KEEPERS ASSOCIATION

The Sable Points Lighthouse Keepers Association (SPLKA) operates four lighthouse stations on Lake Michigan: Big Sable Point, Little Sable Point, Ludington North Breakwater Lighthouses, and White River Light Station.

Each property offers a Lighthouse Keeper Program for members of the public from May- October of each year. They offer clean and very comfortable accommodations at the Ludington State Park and Silver Lake State Park for those interested in the program. During your 1-2 week term of service, you can enjoy beautiful forests and magnificent sand dunes, while helping to preserve and promote a historic property.

SPLKA seeks to preserve, promote and educate the general public on the lighthouse history and make them open for public access. They invite the public to become members of SPLKA for a small donation and take part in the Resident Keeper Program at one of their four beautiful lighthouses at Big Sable, Little Sable, Ludington North Breakwater Light and White River Light Station.

Lighthouse Keepers with SPLKA serve for a specific tour of duty, lasting either one or two weeks. At Big Sable Point this time is set for two weeks where the keepers live on-site in the keeper quarters on the upper floor of the house. For Little Sable Point the typical tour of duty is just one weeklong and the keeper will stay in a residence at the Silver Lake State Park. For Ludington North Breakwater Lighthouse, the typical tour of duty is also one weeklong, and keepers will stay in a residence at Ludington State Park. Lighthouse Keepers are also needed for weekend coverage at the White River Lighthouse location.

Main Duties

• Complete training and education on the history of the lighthouse.
• Greeting visitors and answering questions.
• General upkeep of the lighthouse and grounds
• Provide tours to the public.
• Gift shop and admissions sales.
• Selling SPLKA merchandise.

Things To Know

• Must be 18 years or older.
• Pets are not allowed for these positions.
• White River Lighthouse does not provide lodging.
• Membership is $60 per person or $100 per couple for a full year.

Contact Info

Web: www.splka.org

Email: splkaoperations@gmail.com
Call: 231-845-7417

WORKAMPING AS A VOLUNTEER

Exploring the country from the seat of a motorhome is a picture-perfect way to travel around this country and experience many of the beautiful landscapes, destinations, and local attractions.

As RVers, we have the unparalleled privilege to explore on a different level in the places and spaces we choose to call home for undetermined amounts of time.

Employers from east to west and north to south welcome caravans of seasonal, part-time and full-time RVers to come stay and play at their business throughout the best seasons of the year, while we earn our keep and some cash for more travels down the road.

2 WAYS TO VOLUNTEER WHILE RVING

Volunteering as an RVer can open the doors of travel. Different from a site exchange, where you are required to work a set number of hours to an employer to cover the cost of your site

and utilities, volunteering refers to the gifting of time and energy to a non-profit organization or a government run entity, such as the US Army Corp of Engineers. We typically see two ways of volunteering that fit the workamping lifestyle.

Some RVers choose to travel strictly by volunteering, giving back, and helping those in need for reasons beyond this article text and those close to their hearts.

They have reliable sources of monthly income and the means to sustain their travels without the need for additional income from workamping and can thus donate their time in exchange for great adventures. This is a great option for those who don't want to earn too much income and possibly risk their retirement income or social security benefits.

Other RVers will find that a mixture of both paying positions and those strictly volunteering is the best fit for their lifestyle. Working at least one volunteer position throughout the year, in addition to other paid gigs-give a variety to travel and allows for money to be made when and where needed.

This combination style of workamping is more easily attainable and many RVers find this is the happy place where goodwill, free camping, and great adventures seem to all blend!

FLEXIBLE & REWARDING

As a volunteer, the work is often more flexible in shifts, responsibilities, and length of commitment.

You'll be helping an organization of your choice achieve its goals and mission, while giving your days some structure and keeping busy. It's also a great way to grow your resume for future positions down the road.

We should commend those who are willing and able to volunteer while out exploring and finding new adventures, and maybe look to broaden our own horizons, if you're like me and have not yet taken on a volunteer workamping position.

However, you choose, volunteering will still deliver the main benefits of workamping, freedom of location while living with reduced expenses and the opportunity to discover new and exciting places with enough time to explore like a local!

VOLUNTEER POSITIONS TO CONSIDER

Disney Wilderness Preserve

The Nature Conservancy's 11,500-acre Disney Wilderness Preserve is located in central Fl. and hires friendly, experienced, and conservation-minded couples to help with its mission.

Choose to volunteer for up to 6-months, with a 3-month minimum from October to April.

A FHU campsite will be provided for 32 hours of volunteer work per week. Volunteer work may consist of carpentry, vehicle maintenance, road and trail maintenance, janitorial duties, office work, and visitor center duties.

Contact Dan Cole at: 407-935-0002, ext 126 or dcole@tnc.org

LowerNine.org

A nonprofit organization rebuilding homes in the Lower Ninth Ward of New Orleans from the flooding that resulted from Hurricane Katrina back in 2005.

They will provide all the necessary project training, tools, and safety equipment for work to be done. No previous construction experience is needed to apply.

Projects can include any of the following: roofing and framing, installation of windows and doors, drywall, tile work, interior painting, replacing siding, painting and yard work.

Volunteers can choose their length of service! Work for one day, one year, or anything in between! Work is available year-round.

Contact: emily@lowernine.org

Community First! Village

The Community First! Village lifts the homeless off the streets and into restored RVs.

The 27-acre community in East Austin, TX is looking for folks to assist in restoring used RVs and responding to requests for repairs.

25 hours of work per week is required in exchange for an RV site and utilities.

Contact: Kevin@mlf.org

The Neal Taylor Nature Center

The Neal Taylor Nature Center hires camp hosts. Duties may include greeting visitors, office work, and cleaning.

Strong computer skills and/or outside maintenance experience is highly desirable.

Work 20 hours per week for a FHU site.

Contact: Julie at: 805-693-0691 or email: julie@clnaturecenter.org

Castle Dome Museum

The Castle Dome Museum and hull mine natural wonder florescent mineral wall accept volunteers.

Work just 3 days per week for FHU by large Solar Arrays. Be a part of a spectacular underground tour and wild west museum.

Located right outside Yuma, AZ. in Kofa National Wildlife area.

www.Castledomemuseum.org

Barberville Pioneer Settlement

Step back in time at Barberville Pioneer Settlement and teach school children about the days of yonder.

You'll love the friendly, peaceful atmosphere while demonstrating the lost trades like candle making, wood working, weaving and even blacksmithing.

Other duties can include the usual groundskeeping, light cleaning, general maintenance, and also some clerical duties.

Work. 20 hours per week per person. FHU provided. Background screenings required.

Contact: directors@pioneersettlement.org

YMCA Camp Sequoia Lake

Volunteer at the YMCA Camp Sequoia Lake (singles or couples)! You'll help by working in the kitchens serving kids and families.

Full hookup campsite or on-site housing provided, plus all meals.

Contact Simon at 559-624-1110 simonh@campsequoialake.org

Pisgah Hospitality Partners

Enjoy several campgrounds located in Pisgah National Park, between Asheville to Brevard. They are looking for friendly couples as Volunteer Hosts during the spring/summer seasons!

The host work-exchange program involves working designated hours during each week for a FHU site. A 3-month commitment or longer is required. Host season starts March 15 and runs through October 30.

Contact: info@pisgahcampgrounds.com 828-552-8040, ext. 5.

Battery Point Lighthouse

The Battery Point Lighthouse hires volunteers to work as day tour guides and gift shop staff.

Commitments are 1 month long each and an RV site is provided during the time of service.

Located in Crescent City, California – 20 miles south of the Oregon border, near Redwood National and State Parks.

Contact:manager@delnortehistory.org

IDAHO STATE PARKS

Volunteers have been helping to bring the Idaho State Park Host Program closer to its mission of providing quality recreation opportunities to guests for about 50 years. Each volunteer, regardless of their position, plays a critical part in allowing the program to meet its goals on day to day operations as well as specialized programs.

There are many different ways to volunteer your time inside the Idaho State Parks including Maintenance Hosts, Visitor Services Hosts, Interpretive Host, Special Projects and the popular Campground Host position that is so well known throughout the RVing community.

In most cases, the volunteer hosts live and work onsite in recreational vehicles, although sometimes additional accommodations can be made.

STATE PARK POSITIONS

Campground Hosts

Campground Hosts are considered park ambassadors who live and work inside the park's campground. Every host needs to have a friendly disposition, an outgoing personality, and be genuinely helpful and courteous to all park visitors. They play an integral part in greeting visitors, providing information to the public, and working with the rangers regarding issues inside the park.

Campground Hosts will have a variety of routine tasks such as answering questions and providing local tourist information, checking voicemails and accepting incoming calls, locking and unlocking park buildings, checking the campground daily, making reservations, working in the Visitor Center, as well as cleaning restrooms and picking up litter throughout the park grounds.

A typical schedule will include a variety of days and times but will usually include 24-30 hours of service.

Time commitments between 30-180 days are typical and they have positions for singles, as well as couples throughout the season. Although specific dates and times will be schedule for each host to work, you will be considered 'on-call' at all times of the day and night and they request that you take days off Monday - Thursday.

Visitor Services Host

Visitor Service Hosts are volunteers who answer questions and provide information to park visitors at park entrances and/or inside the visitor centers.

Working as clerks in the parks' retail stores, helping with clerical and front desk receptionist duties, as well as other tasks like posting information on the park's bulletin boards, conducting informational tours of the exhibits, assisting with group scheduling and school field trips, as well as maintaining inventory of merchandise in gift stores.

Hosts in this role benefit from computer and secretarial skills which can be used to help park personnel do various reporting procedures, keep records and reorder supplies. Visitor

Service Hosts work a minimum of 24 hours a week, which can sometimes include weekends and holiday.

Interpretive Hosts

Interpretive Hosts are park trained volunteers who have the unique job of interpreting the natural, cultural and recreational resources available to state park visitors.

Volunteers in this role will greet visitors, sell tickets to exhibited areas, and give short presentations to orient park guests on the specific exhibits and facilities. Knowledge of the history pertaining to the Oregon Trail is helpful in this position, but not necessarily required.

Interpretive Hosts work a minimum of 24 hours a week, which can sometimes include weekends and holidays. Continued on-site training is available in this role and you are encouraged to add your own custom approach with the delivery of the material to make it your own.

Maintenance Hosts

Maintenance Hosts assist in the minor repair and maintenance of state park facilities and grounds. Existing buildings and other structures need cleaning, painting, repairing, and improvements on an ongoing basis making this position a labor-intensive role that takes some special skills.

Sought after skills include electrical, carpentry, painting, masonry, landscaping, and small motor repair.

The Maintenance Hosts' job duties will include trail maintenance, facility construction, plumbing and electrical jobs, sanding and painting picnic tables, running errands when necessary, cleaning public restrooms, stocking bird feeders, removing litter from walkways, as well as mowing, trimming vegetation, weed removal, mulching and operating the irrigation systems throughout the park. The Maintenance Hosts can also help park staff on new construction projects if necessary.

In this role, you can expect to work at least 20 hours a week for a minimum 30 days. A state vehicle will be provided for work-related driving needs and you will also have support evaluations on job performance throughout your commitment.

VOLUNTEER BENEFITS

Volunteering in one of Idaho State Parks can be a very rewarding experience that comes with an array of non-monetary benefits from being part of the community. Whether you are planting trees, teaching safe boating practices, providing insight on an exhibit, restoring a historic area, building a trail, assisting campers, or answering public inquiries, Idaho State Park volunteers will have the following benefits:

• Full or partial hook up campground
• All access pass to all Idaho State Parks
• Uniform provided for all volunteers
• Learning historical information about the area.
• Formal and informal recognition for a job well done.
• Gain valuable skills and work experience.
• An opportunity to maintain skills you've previously mastered.
• Strengthen your social ties to the community and fellow RVers.
• Chances to meet new people and interact with a diverse group of guests.

When considering if a host position is right for you, you'll need to make sure you are 100% capable and willing to complete the duties and tasks associated with it.

Consider your physical limitations and how they may or may not play a part in your daily job responsibilities. Don't hesitate to ask questions during the hiring process to make sure you're comfortable with the job and the area. Then, once you're on site take some time to get oriented to the area so you'll be better suited to share your personal insight with future guests.

As part of the volunteer program at Idaho State Parks, all hosts are asked to meet the following expectations:

• Agree to job duties as outline on the signed Volunteer Service Agreement.
• Show up for your schedule shifts on time and carry out your job as described.
• Stay through the time frame you've committed to and allow for a replacement to be found if you need to leave early.
• Maintain a clean, uncluttered and orderly campsite at all times, where additional storage and structures are not added, and plants or gardens are grown in portable containers.
• Dress appropriately in uniform and refrain from consuming alcohol or use tobacco while on active duty.
• Avoid offensive language and conduct at all times.
• Keep dogs on a leash and have current rabies certificates.

If you are interested in a position as a host for Idaho State Parks, consider working at one of the locations listed below who still have openings for the 2019 peak season.

This list will provide an overview of the location's peak season, electrical service available at the host sites, as well as what type of positions they currently have available.

STATE PARK SEASON AVAILABILITY

Billingsley Creek March – Oct. 50 Maintenance, Visitor Services, Special Projects

Bruneau Dunes March – Nov 30 Visitor Services Host

Castle Rocks May – Oct. 50 Maintenance, Interpretive Host, Visitor Services

Smokey Mtn CG May – Oct. 50 Campground Host

Dworshak May – Oct. 30 Maintenance, Campground Host, Visitor Services

Eagle Island May – Oct. 50 Maintenance, Special Projects

Harriman June – Oct 50 Interpretive Host, Visitor Services, Special Projects

Henrys Lake May – Sept 50 Campground Host, Visitor Services Host

Heyburn May – Oct. 30 Maintenance, Campground Host

Lake Cascade May – Sept. 50 Campground Host, Interpretive Host

Lake Walcott May – Sept. 30
Campground Host

Malad Gorge April – Oct. 50
Maintenance, Visitor Services

Massacre Rocks April – Oct. 30
Maintenance, Campground Host,
Interpretive Host, Visitor Services,
Special Projects

Priest Lake May – Oct. 50 Visitor
Services Host

Ritter Island April – Oct 50
Maintenance, Interpretive Host,
Visitor Services, Special Projects

FOR MORE INFORMATION

Contact Idaho State Parks

Email: idprvolunteer@idpr.idaho.gov

Website:https://parksandrecreation.i
daho.gov/activities/volunteering

Call: (208) 514-2493

MT RAINIER NATIONAL PARK RV JOBS

Any experience working at a National Park- can be life changing, and while I'm a big fan of the workamping program by at Yellowstone by Delaware North- I wanted to take a minute to talk about the workamping program at Mount Rainier, since I'm currently located just a few hours east of it!

This program is championed by Rainier Guest Services, which operate several properties including the Jackson Visitor Center, National Park Inn and the Paradise Inn as a concessioner for the National Park Service with jobs available in food service, gift shops, lodging, and customer service!

Although the park operates year-round their main season, which offers the most workamping jobs runs from April through October. They have a team of over 240 employees each season, that help to provide visitors with exceptional experiences and create wonderful memories.

As part of the team at Mount Rainier National Park, you'll have the opportunity to really enjoy the surrounding area during your stay in Washington state!

Since large parts of the property are surrounded by National Forest, it really provides some exception recreation right outside your doorstep including exploring the Colombia River Gorge, Mount St. Helens National Volcanic Area and the entire Puget Sound region which holds awesome tourist attractions including the Space Needle and Pike Place Market right in Seattle!

RV LIFE AT MT. RAINIER NP

If you love the outdoors and can deal with being over 60 miles from a major city with limited modern services than workamping at Mount Rainier might be for you! Employees are welcomed to live and work in a rustic mountain setting where cell phone signals are literally non-existent and wi-fi is slow at best.

Opportunities to explore the area are a huge draw for this workamping job, with outdoor experiences that seem almost limitless. With the tallest volcano as well as the most glaciated peak in the continental United States, Mount Rainier draws in an incredible amount of families, hikers, photographers, and nature lovers from all around the world.

WORKAMPING RAINIER GUEST SERVICES

The main workamping season runs from mid-April through min-October. They hire for a variety of different positions, which are all listed in detail on their website. All RVers are expected to work a variety of hours and days, but in general schedules will include weekends and holidays.

Schedules are not guaranteed, nor or the number of hours per worker but you can expect to work between 35-40 hours per week.

When applying for a position, you will provide information on when you are able to start work and when you will need to leave. These dates will play a large part in the HR teams' decision on whether they are able to offer you a position to join the workamping team,

so make sure the information you provide is as accurate as possible.

If you are available to work for the entire season you might have a better chance of being hired than those who are only available for smaller time frames.

Benefits of workamping at Rainier Guest Services include an employee discount inside the retail locations as well as several scheduled employee events throughout the prime season. Full-time RVers will greatly appreciate the benefit of being provided with FREE laundry facilities, which is a big plus in my book!

Committed to providing a drug-free workplace, you will be both- drug tested once you arrive as well as subject to random drug testing throughout the workamping season. Failure will result in termination of employment.

WORKAMPER RV SITES

RV sites are offered at two specific locations while workamping at Mt. Rainier, both offering 30amp hook-ups.

One location is inside the park and offers a wooded campground setting, the other is outside the park next to the administrative office and provides a quiet scenic area. Shower facilities and bathrooms are not offered at either location, so all RVs must be self-contained.

Longmire Campground

is located inside the park near the National Park Inn. This location is a beautifully wooded campground for public guests and holds typically 6-8 RV sites. It offers soil pads and includes a laundry facility and Wi-Fi that is about ½ a mile away. Water/Sewer/ and 30amp electricity is available for RVers, but cell service is not available, and they cannot accommodate larger model RV units. Cost for the RV site is just $30 weekly for employee.

Ashford Campground

is located just 5 minutes outside the National Park. It offers a quiet, scenic camping experience with 13 additional sites for RVers.

RV sites here, are cement pads that include water/sewer and 30amp electricity. Wi-Fi is free at this location and it also includes an onsite laundry facility. Staff will pay $60 per week for camping at Ashford Campground.

At both locations, Mount Rainier Guest Service allows the presence of well-behaved cats and dogs that are less than 30lbs. They set a max. of 1 pet per RV and all animals must be kept on a leash at all times when outside your RV and cannot be left unattended.

WORKAMPING WITHOUT AN RV

Mount Rainier National Park offers onsite housing for those wishing to work without an RV, or maybe those who just want to switch it up and try dorm life! Dorms provide basic accommodations for RVers where several employees will share one room.

If you are thinking about applying for a position with Rainier Guest Services to work at Mount Rainier National Park and live in company provide housing, keep in mind that applicants have to be at least 18 years old.

AVAILABLE POSITIONS

There are tons of available positions through the workamping program by Rainier Guest Services, but I just pulled in some information for a few I thought were pretty interesting. Here are some job descriptions of possible jobs for RVers that can be found on their website including many, many more!

Retail Clerk

Retail Sales Associates is responsible for assisting customers in making purchases in a friendly, accurate and efficient manner.

The Retail Sales Associate is also responsible for merchandising and creating displays, cleanliness, product presentation, receiving money from and disbursing money to customers, and maintaining a high level of customer service at all times.

Housekeeper

The Housekeeper performs routine daily tasks in a safe and efficient manner to clean guest rooms, public restrooms, and public areas of the hotel, including stripping and making beds, cleaning bathrooms, and vacuuming hallways.

Lead Cook

The Lead Cook, under the direction of the Executive Chef, prepares, cooks, and serves food in a three meal per day Dining Room serving up to 1,200 covers per, that are nutritious, safe, wholesome, eye appealing, delicious, and meet recipe and food cost specifications. Perform culinary functions at a higher skill level and efficiency than Line Cook.

Front Desk Agent

The Front Desk Agent must have the ability to perform all desk attendant functions including provide excellent service at the hotel front desk, performing all relevant functions including checking guests in and out, completing reservations, answering phones, coordinating services for guests.

General Manager

The Manager is responsible for all aspects of unit operation and floor management, including merchandise, equipment, and property to facilitate fulfillment of financial goals, company incentives and client standards. Maintain a consistently high standard of guest service, cleanliness, product presentation, and cost control.

Supervise Retail Lead and Retail Clerks to ensure tasks are completed in a friendly, safe and efficient manner.

Barista

Provide excellent service in the café by serving coffee, specialty drinks, ice cream, and other food items, completing guest transactions in a friendly, accurate, and efficient manner. Maintain a high standard of cleanliness and product presentation.

Baker Assistance

The Baker Assistant assists in the daily production of specialty baked goods at Paradise Inn including pastries and desserts. Assist Lead

Baker by preparing ingredients, following recipes, baking items, and keeping the kitchen clean and orderly.

Busser

The Busser is responsible for assisting the Server to deliver bread, serve water, replenish supplies and assist in maintain the cleanliness of all areas of the restaurant.

Front Desk Agent

The Front Desk Agent must have the ability to perform all desk attendant functions including provide excellent service at the hotel front desk, performing all relevant functions including checking guests in and out, completing reservations, answering phones, coordinating services for guests.

Prep Cook

The Prep Cook assists the Cook by preparing ingredients, keeping the kitchen clean and orderly, and by performing some of the simpler cooking functions as assigned according to the menu.

Laundry Attendant

The Laundry Attendant is responsible for cleaning and sanitizing the facility's linens and guests' laundry as directed. Operate commercial laundry equipment to provide a daily supply of clean linens and employee uniforms for all park operations. Quickly and accurately sort and fold clean laundry by hand. Assist with check-in and check-out of employee uniforms. Cleaning the offices and restrooms in the Administration building.

THINGS YOU NEED TO KNOW:

• Paradise Inn are is at 5,400 feet elevation
• Jackson Visitor Center is at 5,400 feet elevation
• Sunrise Lodge is at 6,400 feet.
• It can snow anytime of the year.
• 60 miles from any major city.
• Cell phone signals are non-existent
• Summer temperatures are typically moderate.
• Jackson Visitor Center positions need to be filled from mid-April to mid-October.
• Ashford Warehouse positions need to be filled from mid-April to mid-October.
• Paradise Inn positions will need to be staffed from mid-May to early October.
• Sunrise Lodge positions will need to be staffed from late June to early September.

WORKAMPING APPLICATION PROCESS

If you are interested in workamping at Mount Rainier National Park- contact Rainier Guest Services by filling out an online application.

Due to the amount of applications received, they cannot guarantee you will be contacted if not a fit for an open position. If chosen to move forward, you will be contacted for a phone interview. Once hired, you'll receive a Work agreement via email with more details on your position for the upcoming season.

SECTION 3

EMPLOYER INFORMATION

The key to a successful Live Camp Work lifestyle is having an arsenal of reliable employers and business opportunities! Regardless of if you intend to work seasonally, part-time or full-time you will need ample information on who is hiring, when they hire and what positions they usually have available.

I suggest starting your own spreadsheet to keep track of this information and help you maintain necessary insight on specific employers for future reference. This can be as simple as just listing the employer name, contact information, and notes in 3 separate columns or as elaborate as you want with dates, pay and other information.

To help you get started I've provided employer information on over 1000 companies that hire RVers in this book!

I haven't done all the work for you, but I've given the employer name and at least one piece of contact information to enable you to start your research.

A word of caution: I've done my best to search for employers and information that made note of hiring RVers in some capacity. I did not contact each employer or contact listed for details or relevance.

If you plan to reach out to any employers, it is my strong suggestion that you first look up their websites to find some general information. After you are confident in your findings and want to inquire about possible openings, you could then send an initial email with an introduction and inquiry for information and steps to move forward!

THE US FOREST SERVICE

The US Forest Service manages over 150 national forests and 20 grasslands in the US and Puerto Rico! Your experience can be put to good use by volunteering with the Forest Service in almost any position, outside of law enforcement and firefighting. As a volunteer, you will be one of over 2.8 million, since 1972, who have provided over 120 million hours of service!

Paid positions with the US Forest Service may also be available for seasonal and/or temporary jobs, which can be found easily online at https://www.fs.fed.us/working-with-us/jobs. As a volunteer you will also have the opportunity to earn an America the Beautiful National Parks & Federal Recreation Lands Pass for your service.

Make sure if you are interested in a volunteer position with the US Forest Service that you browse the open positions on www.Volunteer.gov and also contact the appropriate Program Specialist from the list below directly with your questions.

NATIONAL HEADQUARTERS

Includes Washington, D.C.

Contact: Merlene Mazyck
National Program Manager
mmazyck@fs.fed.us

Contact: Keyana Ellis Reynolds
Program Coordinator
keyanaellis@fs.fed.us

NORTHERN REGION

Includes Montana, Idaho, North Dakota, South Dakota, and Washington.

Contact: Joni Packard
406-329-3187
jpackard@fs.fed.us

ROCKY MOUNTAIN REGION

Colorado, Wyoming, South Dakota, Nebraska

Contact: Kristin Schmitt
303-275-5384
kristinschmitt@fs.fed.us

SOUTHWESTERN REGION

Includes Arizona, New Mexico, Oklahoma and Texas

Contact: Jennifer Nelson
505-842-3441
jennifernelson@fs.fed.us

INTERMOUNTAIN REGION

Includes Utah, Wyoming, Idaho, Nevada and California

Contact: Bill Lyons
801-625-5458
blyons@fs.fed.us

PACIFIC SOUTHWEST REGION

Includes California and Hawaii

Contact: Kathy Mick
707-562-8859
kmick@fs.fed.us

PACIFIC NORTHWEST REGION

Includes Washington and Oregon

Contact: Emily Biesecker
503-808-2816
ebiesecker@fs.fed.us

SOUTHERN REGION

Includes Alabama, Arkansas, Florida, Georgia, Kentucky, Louisiana, Mississippi, North Carolina, Oklahoma, Puerto Rico, South Carolina, Tennessee, Texas, and Virginia

Contact: Michelle Mitchell
404-347-1749
michellemitchell@fs.fed.us

SOUTHERN RESEARCH STATION

Includes Alabama, Arkansas, Florida, Georgia, Kentucky, Louisiana, Mississippi, North Carolina, Oklahoma, Puerto Rico, South Carolina, Tennessee, Texas, and Virginia

Contact: Joyce Gorgas
828-257-4281
jgorgas@fs.fed.us

EASTERN REGION

Includes Connecticut, Delaware, Illinois, Indiana, Iowa, Maine, Maryland, Massachusetts, Michigan, Minnesota, Missouri, New Hampshire, New Jersey, New York, Ohio, Pennsylvania, Rhode Island, Vermont, West Virginia, and Wisconsin

Contact: Dawn Meier
715-362-1386
dmeier@fs.fed.us

ALASKA REGION

Includes Alaska

Contact: George Schaaf
907-586-7876
gschaaf@fs.fed.us

STATE PARK PROGRAM INFORMATION

Included below is the best website address for seasonal employment and volunteer opportunities available for each state park volunteer system. This should serve as your starting point when searching for jobs inside the state park systems. If you have questions regarding specific positions or parks, contact that park individual to find out the most updated information on how to apply.

ALABAMA STATE PARKS

www.alapark.com/volunteering

ALASKA STATE PARKS

www.dnr.state.ak.us/parks/vip

ARIZONA STATE PARKS

www.azstateparks.com/employment

www.azstateparks.com/volunteer

ARKANSAS STATE PARKS

www.arkansasstateparks.com/about/employment

CALIFORNIA STATE PARKS

www.livetheparkslife.com

COLORADO STATE PARKS

www.cpw.state.co.us/aboutus/Pages/Jobs.aspx

CONNECTICUT STATE PARKS

www.ct.gov/deep/jobs

DELAWARE STATE PARKS

www.destateparks.com/Volunteer/VolunteerHosting

www.destateparks.com/GetInvolved/JoinOurStaff

FLORIDA STATE PARKS

www.floridastateparks.org/getinvolved/volunteer

GEORGIA STATE PARKS

http://explore.gastateparks.org/volunteer

www.gastateparks.org/ParkCareers

IDAHO STATE PARKS

www.parksandrecreation.idaho.gov/activities/volunteering

www.parksandrecreation.idaho.gov/seasonal-employment-idaho-state-parks-0

ILLINOIS STATE PARKS

www.dnr.illinois.gov/outreach/Volunteer

INDIANA STATE PARKS

www.in.gov/dnr/parklake/2443.htm

www.indianainnsjobs.com

www.in.gov/dnr/parklake/2439.htm

IOWA DEPARTMENT OF NATURAL RESOURCES

www.iowadnr.gov/About-DNR/Volunteer-Opportunities

KANSAS DEPARTMENT OF WILDLIFE & PARKS

https://ksoutdoors.com/KDWPT-Info/Jobs/Current-KDWPT-Employment-Opportunities/Volunteer-Opportunities

https://ksoutdoors.com/KDWPT-Info/Jobs/Current-KDWPT-Employment-Opportunities/Seasonal-and-Temporary-Positions

KENTUCKY DEPARTMENT OF PARKS

www.parks.ky.gov/volunteer/

LOUISIANA OFFICE OF STATE PARKS

www.crt.state.la.us/louisiana-state-parks/campground-host/index

www.crt.state.la.us/employment-opportunities/

MAINE STATE PARKS

www.maine.gov/dacf/parks/get_involved/volunteer.shtml

www.maine.gov/dacf/parks/get_involved/employment_opportunities.shtml

MARYLAND STATE PARKS

www.jobapscloud.com/MD/#EmpDiv55

www.dnr.maryland.gov/Pages/volunteer.aspx

MASSACHUSETTS DIVISION OF FORESTS & PARKS

www.mass.gov/service-details/learn-about-host-camping

www.mass.gov/service-details/volunteers-in-the-parks

MICHIGAN STATE PARKS

www.michigan.gov/dnr/

MINNESOTA DEPARTMENT OF NATURAL RESOURCES

www.dnr.state.mn.us/volunteering

www.dnr.state.mn.us/jobs

MISSISSIPPI STATE PARKS

www.mdwfp.com/museum/see-visit/volunteer/

MISSOURI DEPARTMENT OF NATURAL RESOURCES

www.mostateparks.com/page/55061/employment-opportunities

www.mostateparks.com/page/57872/volunteer-parks-program

MONTANA STATE PARKS

www.stateparks.mt.gov/volunteer/

NEBRASKA GAME & PARKS COMMISSION

www.outdoornebraska.gov/volunteer/

NEVADA STATE PARKS

http://parks.nv.gov/about/volunteer-and-support

http://parks.nv.gov/about/employment

NEW HAMPSHIRE STATE PARKS

www.nhstateparks.org/about-us/support/volunteer.aspx

www.nhstateparks.org/about-us/employment-opportunities.aspx

NEW JERSEY PARKS & FORESTRY

www.state.nj.us/dep/parksandforests/parks/volunteers.html

www.state.nj.us/dep/parksandforests/parks/jobs.html

NEW MEXICO STATE PARKS

http://www.emnrd.state.nm.us/SPD/Volunteering.html

NEW YORK STATE PARKS

https://parks.ny.gov/employment/

NORTH CAROLINA STATE PARKS

www.ncparks.gov/volunteer

www.ncparks.gov/Jobs/seasonal

NORTH DAKOTA PARKS & RECREATION DEPT.

http://www.parkrec.nd.gov/information/department/employment.html

OHIO STATE PARKS

http://ohiodnr.gov/contact/volunteer-with-odnr

OREGON PARKS & RECREATION DEPARTMENT

https://oregonstateparks.org/index.cfm?do=getinvolved.dsp_volunteer

PENNSYLVANIA STATE PARKS

www.dcnr.pa.gov/GetInvolved

RHODE ISLAND STATE PARKS

www.riparks.com/Employment.html

SOUTH CAROLINA STATE PARK SERVICE

www.scprt.com/state-park-service/volunteeropportunities

https://www.scprt.com/parks/jobs-at-state-parks/temporary-and-seasonal-employment

SOUTH DAKOTA PARKS & RECREATION

https://gfp.sd.gov/volunteer/

https://gfp.sd.gov/seasonal/

TENNESSEE STATE PARKS AND RECREATION

https://tnstateparks.com/get-involved/volunteering

TEXAS PARKS AND WILDLIFE

https://tpwd.texas.gov/state-parks/help-parks/
https://tpwd.texas.gov/jobs/state_parks/

UTAH PARKS AND RECREATION

https://stateparks.utah.gov/resources/volunteer/

https://naturalresources.utah.gov/seasonal-employment

VERMONT STATE PARKS

https://vtstateparks.com/employment.html

https://vtstateparks.com/volunteering.html

VIRGINIA STATE PARKS

http://www.dcr.virginia.gov/state-parks/camp-host

http://www.dcr.virginia.gov/jobs

WASHINGTON STATE PARKS

http://parks.state.wa.us/262/Volunteer-Program

http://parks.state.wa.us/774/Jobs

WISCONSIN STATE PARKS

https://www.dnr.state.wi.us/topic/parks/volunteer.html

WYOMING STATE PARKS AND HISTORIC SITES

http://wyoparks.state.wy.us/index.php/learn/volunteer-opportunities

EMPLOYERS WITH ONSITE HOUSING

If you haven't purchased an RV yet or you would just like an adventure that provides onsite housing options, the following list is provided for Employers who provide room and board for staff.

You will need to verify if housing is provided free of charge or if fees are required. You might also want to verify the meal options available onsite as well.

DENALI PARK RESORTS

https://www.denaliparkvillage.com

YMCA OF THE ROCKIES

http://www.workintherockies.org

HOTEL IROQUOIS

http://www.iroquoishotel.com/

employment@iroquoishotel.com

ISLE ROYALE RESORTS, LLC

http://www.rockharborlodge.com

IDAHO ROCKY MOUNTAIN RANCH

http://www.idahorocky.com/employment/

info@idahorocky.com

FLATHEAD LAKE LODGE

http://www.flatheadlakelodge.com/

hr@flatheadlakelodge.com

ALTA PERUVIAN LODGE

http://www.altaperuvian.com/

THE LODGE AT BRYCE CANYON

http://www.brycecanyonforever.com/

SOMBRERO STABLES

www.sombrero.com/faqs/employment-with-sombrero/

jobs@sombrero.com

SIGNAL MOUNTAIN LODGE

http://www.workatsignal.com/

ADIRONDACK MOUNTAIN CLUB

http://www.adk.org/

jobs@adk.org

GRAND CANYON NORTH RIM

http://www.grandcanyonforever.com/

gnrhr@gcnr.com

ANDREW AIRWAYS

http://www.andrewairways.com

DEER VALLEY RESORT

http://deervalley.com/jobs

jobs@deervalley.com

KENAI FJORDS WILDERNESS LODGE

http://www.alaskacollection.com/corporate/careers/

HEART 6 RANCH

http://www.heartsix.com/

THE LODGES OF THE NORTHERN BIG HORN MOUNTAINS

http://lodgesofthenorthernbighornmountains.com/

CHISOS MOUNTAINS LODGE

http://chisosmountainslodge.com/

YELLOWSTONE FOREVER

https://www.yellowstone.org/

1000 ADDITIONAL EMPLOYERS

Employer Name	Contact Information
5 Branches Camperpark	co5branches@aol.com
7A Ranch	info@7aranch.co
Abiquiu Lake	austin.c.kuhlman@usace.army.mil
Acadia National Park	jodi.moore@exploreacadia.com
Alabama River Lake	kelli.m.little@usace.army.mil
Alabama River Lakes/Claiborne Lake	jason.r.swanner@usace.army.mil
Alafia River State Park	https://volunteers.floridastateparks.org
Alamo Lake State Park	bworman@azstateparks.gov
Alamo Rose RV Resort	https://www.rvresorts.com/alamo-rose.html
Alaskax	jobs@alaskax.com
Albee Creek Campground	blair.pubols@parks.ca.gov
Albeni Falls Dam/ Lake Pend Oreille	craig.s.brengle@usace.army.mil
Alfred B. Maclay Gardens State Park	https://volunteers.floridastateparks.org
Allatoona Lake	christopher.r.purvis@usace.army.mil
Allen David Broussard Catfish Creek Preserve State Park	https://volunteers.floridastateparks.org

Alta Lake State Park	volunteers@parks.wa.gov
Alum Creek Lake	robert.j.wattenschaidt@usace.army.mil
Amazon Camperforce	www.amazon.com/camperforce
Amelia Island State Park	https://volunteers.floridastateparks.org
American Land & Leisure	www.americanll.com
Ames Brook Campground	barbara@amesbrook.com
Anastasia State Park	https://volunteers.floridastateparks.org
Anchorage RV Park	cmeier@bestofalaskatravel.com
Anclote Key Preserve State Park	https://volunteers.floridastateparks.org
Andersen's Oceanside Resort	http://andersensrv.com
Anderson Lake State Park	bill.drath@parks.wa.gov
Anderson's Landing	https://volunteers.floridastateparks.org
Andrew Molera State Park	sharon.pieniak@parks.ca.gov
Angel Island State Park	www.angelisland.com
Angeles National Forest	www.americanll.com
Anza-Borrego Desert State Park	norbert.ruhmke@parks.ca.gov
Aramark - Olympic National Park	http://www.olympicnationalparks.com/
Aramark Mesa Verde	http://www.visitmesaverde.com/
Aramark Tahoe Jobs	http://www.zephyrcove.com/
Arkabutla Lake	ernest.e.lentz@usace.army.mil
Arkansas River	michael.d.groves@usace.army.mil

Atchafalaya Basin Floodway	alison.k.hebert@usace.army.mil
Atlanta South RV Park	www.atlantasouthrvresort.com
Atlantic Ridge Preserve State Park	https://volunteers.floridastateparks.org
Atwood Lake	lydia.e.fach@usace.army.mil
Auburn State Recreation Area/Mineral Bar	asra@parks.ca.gov
Avalon State Park	https://volunteers.floridastateparks.org
B. Everett Jordan Dam & Lake	john.h.rochevot@usace.army.mil
Badlands Cedar Pass Lodge	http://cedarpasslodge.com/
Bahia Honda State Park	https://volunteers.floridastateparks.org
Bald Point State Park	https://volunteers.floridastateparks.org
Baldhill Dam /Lake Ashtabula	christopher.m.botz@usace.army.mil
Ball Mountain/Townshend Lake	dale.h.berkness@usace.army.mil
Bardwell Lake	justin.w.hebert@usace.army.mil
Barre Falls Dam	brianna.j.green@usace.army.mil
Barren River Lake	holly.l.myers@usace.army.mil
Battle Ground Lake State Park	volunteers@parks.wa.gov
Bay Bayou RV Resort	baybayoumarketing@gmail.com
Bay View State Park	volunteers@parks.wa.gov
Beach City Lake	lydia.e.fach@usace.army.mil

Bear Creek Lake State Park	vspvolunteer@dcr.virginia.gov
Beaver Brook Campground	camp@beaver-brook.com
Beaver Lake	brian.walch@usace.army.mil
Beaver Lake	jared.d.trammell@usace.army.mil
Beech Fork Lake	michael.d.mccomassll@usace.army.mil
Belfair State Park	volunteers@parks.wa.gov
Belle Isle State Park	vspvolunteer@dcr.virginia.gov
Belton/Stillhouse Hollow Lake	arthur.a.johnson@usace.army.mil
Benbow Lake State Recreation Area	christopher.glenn@parks.ca.gov
Benbrook Lake	lyndy.t.black@usace.army.mil
Benicia State Recreation Area	daniel.golde@parks.ca.gov
Bensten Palm RV Park	manager@benstenpalmrvpark.com
Berlin Lake	matthew.j.pook@usace.army.mil
Bethel Outdoor Adventures	info@betheloutdooradventures.com
Bethel Outdoor Adventures and Campground	info@betheloutdooradventure.com
Bidwell-Sacramento River State Park	matthew.stalter@parks.ca.gov
Big Basin State Park	www.bigbasintentcabins.com
Big Lagoon State Park	https://volunteers.floridastateparks.org
Big Shoals State Park	https://volunteers.floridastateparks.org
Big Talbot Island State Park	https://volunteers.floridastateparks.org
Bill Baggs Cape Florida State Park	https://volunteers.floridastateparks.org

Birch Bay State Park	volunteers@parks.wa.gov
Birch Hill Dam	jeffrey.c.mangum@usace.army.mil
Birch Lake	jeffery.a.walker@usace.army.mil
Black Butte Lake	amber.r.machado@usace.army.mil
Black Butte Lake	amber.r.machado@usace.army.mil
Black Hawk Park	eric.m.hammer@usace.army.mil
Black Hills National Forest	fstremgt@aol.com
Black Warrior/Tombigbee Lake	benjamin.h.sherrod@usace.army.mil
Blackwater River Heritage State Trail	https://volunteers.floridastateparks.org
Blackwater River State Park	https://volunteers.floridastateparks.org
Blake Island State Park	volunteers@parks.wa.gov
Blue Marsh Lake	nathan.t.freiwald@usace.army.mil
Blue Mountain Lake	jeremy.e.wells@usace.army.mil
Blue Spring State Park	https://volunteers.floridastateparks.org
Blue Springs Lake and Longview Lake	james.j.dickerson@usace.army.mil
Bluestone Lake	travis.d.daugherty@usace.army.mil
Bogachiel State Park	volunteers@parks.wa.gov
Bolivar Dam	lydia.e.fach@usace.army.mil
Bonnet Carre' Spillway	christopher.g.brantley@usace.army.mil
Bonneville Lock and Dam/Willamette Falls Locks	nicole.l.baker@usace.army.mil
Bothe-Napa Valley State Park	jason.jordon@countyofnapa.org

Bouse RV Park	yp2868@gmail.com
Bowlin Travel Centers	www.bowlintc.com
Boyce Thompson Arboretum State Park	bworman@azstateparks.gov
Brainard Lake Recreation Area	www.americanll.com
Brannan Island SRA	www.americanll.com
Bridgeport State Park	volunteers@parks.wa.gov
Bridle Trails State Park	volunteers@parks.wa.gov
Brooks Memorial State Park	volunteers@parks.wa.gov
Brookville Lake	stephanie.a.ison@usace.army.mil
Buckhorn Lake	priscilla.a.southwood@usace.army.mil
Bucks Lake Camp	rmgrubbs@sbcglobal.net
Buckskin Mountain State Park	bworman@azstateparks.gov
Buena Vista RV Resort	www.buenavistarvresort.com
Buena Vista RV Resort	propertymanager@buenavistarvresort.com
Buffumville Lake/Hodges Village Dam	jamie.r.kordack@usace.army.mil
Building Pro	www.buildingpro.com
Bulow Creek State Park	https://volunteers.floridastateparks.org
Bulow Plantation Ruins Historic State Park	https://volunteers.floridastateparks.org
Burlington Campground	blair.pubols@parks.ca.gov
Burnsville Lake	ryan.s.davis@usace.army.mil
Butano State Park	shawn.wilson@parks.ca.gov

C.J. Brown Dam & Reservoir	brian.t.menker@usace.army.mil
Caesar Creek Lake	russell.r.curtis@usace.army.mil
Cagles Mill Lake	george.c.baker@usace.army.mil
Cal-Am Resorts	http://www.cal-am.com/careers/
Caladesi Island State Park	https://volunteers.floridastateparks.org
Calaveras Big Trees State Park	barry.robertson@parks.ca.gov
California Land Management	www.clm-services.com
Cama Beach State Park	volunteers@parks.wa.gov
Camanche Recreation Company	www.camancherecreation.com
Camano Island State Park	volunteers@parks.wa.gov
Camp Gulf	www.campgulf.com
Camp Hatteras	camphatteras.com
Camp Helen State Park	https://volunteers.floridastateparks.org
Camp Riverview in Concan, TX	info@friocampriverview.com
Camp Wooten State Park	volunteers@parks.wa.gov
Canton Lake	shawna.m.polen@usace.army.mil
Cantwell RV Park	cantwellrvpark.wordpress.com
Canyon Lake	samuell.h.price@usace.army.mil
Cape Camp Resort	capecampresort@aol.com
Cape Cod Canal	elisa.d.carey@usace.army.mil
Cape Cod Maple Park	tonya@capecodmaplepark.com

Cape Disappointment LCIC	volunteers@parks.wa.gov
Cape Disappointment State Park	volunteers@parks.wa.gov
Capps Crossing Campground	www.americanll.com
Carlyle Lake	kim.hammel@usace.army.mil
Carpinteria State Beach	cathleen.wills@parks.ca.gov
Carr Creek Lake	kevin.c.wright@usace.army.mil
Carters Lake	jonathan.r.wise@usace.army.mil
Castle Crags State Park	todd.barto@parks.ca.gov
Catalina State Park	bworman@azstateparks.gov
Cattail Cove State Park	bworman@azstateparks.gov
Cauble Park in Acworth, Georgia	elacher@acworth.org
Cave Country RV Campground	jeff@cavecountryrv.com
Cave Run Lake	anthony.w.orr@usace.army.mil
Cayo Costa State Park	https://volunteers.floridastateparks.org
Cecil M. Harden Lake	gary.j.staigl@usace.army.mil
Cedar Key Museum State Park	https://volunteers.floridastateparks.org
Cedar Key Scrub State Reserve	https://volunteers.floridastateparks.org
Center Hill Lake	sarah.j.peace@usace.army.mil
Central Oregon KOA	madrasKOA@msn.com
Charles Mill Lake	bryan.r.muroski@usace.army.mil
Charlotte Harbor Preserve State Park	https://volunteers.floridastateparks.org
Cheatham Lake	roger.d.austin@usace.army.mil

Chena River Lake (Chena Flood Control Project)	stewart.j.gilmore@usace.army.mil
Cherry Valley Campground	www.americanll.com
Chief Joseph Dam/Rufus Woods Lake	theresa.a.poulson@nws.usace.army.mil
China Flat Campground	www.americanll.com
Chippokes Plantation State Park	vspvolunteer@dcr.virginia.gov
Choice Hotels Gardiner, Montana	gm.mt411@choicehotels.com
Chouteau Lock & Dam	joshua.w.mathis@usace.army.mil
Christmas Decor Of Knoxville	http://christmasdecor.net/knoxville
Cider House Campground	www.ciderhousecampground.com
Circle K Guest Ranch	www.ckranch.com
Clackamas County Park	tomgra@co.clakamas.or.us
Clair Tappaan Lodge	www.clairtappaanlodge.com
Clarence Cannon Dam and Mark Twain Lake	mary.a.heitmeyer@usace.army.mil
Claytor Lake State Park	vspvolunteer@dcr.virginia.gov
Clear Lake State Park	darin.conner@parks.ca.gov
Clearwater Lake	donald.henson@usace.army.mil
Clendening Lake, Piedmont Lake, Senecaville Lake, & Tappan Lake	lynette.m.christiansen@usace.army.mil
Clinton Lake	kipp.j.walters@usace.army.mil

Cochiti Lake	william.t.wallin@usace.army.mil
Cochiti Lake Campground	william.t.wallin@usace.army.mil
Cockroach Bay Preserve State Park	https://volunteers.floridastateparks.org
Coconino National Forest	www.coconinonationalforest.us
Coconino National Forest	tgreen01@fs.fed.us
Cold Brook Lake/Cottonwood Springs	kody.l.green@usace.army.mil
Collier-Seminole State Park	https://volunteers.floridastateparks.org
Colorado Parks & Wildlife	www.cpw.state.co.us
Colorado Parks and Wildlife	cpw.volunteer@state.co.us
Colt Creek State Park	https://volunteers.floridastateparks.org
Columbia Hills State Park	volunteers@parks.wa.gov
Columbia Plateau Trail State Park	volunteers@parks.wa.gov
Columbia State Park	volunteers@parks.wa.gov
Conchas Dam	ryan.j.poland@usace.army.mil
Conconully State Park	volunteers@parks.wa.gov
Conemaugh River Lake	april.l.richards@usace.army.mil
Constitution Convention Museum State Park	https://volunteers.floridastateparks.org
Cooper Dam/Jim Chapman Lake	dean.attaway@usace.army.mil
Copan Lake	matthew.k.schuffenhauer@usace.army.mil

Copano Bay RV Resort	www.copanobayrvresort.com
Coralville Lake	leah.c.deeds@usace.army.mil
Cordell Hull Lake	james.s.gregory@usace.army.mil
Corinth Recreation Area	www.americanll.com
Cottage Grove Lake	donna.r.bryant@usace.army.mil
Cottonwood Cove	cottonwood.cove@yahoo.com
Council Grove Lake	mieko.g.alley@usace.army.mil
Cove State Park	volunteers@parks.wa.gov
Coyote Valley Dam	poppy.l.lozoff@usace.army.mil
Cradle of Forestry IA	www.cfaia.org
Crater Lake Lodge - Xanterra	http://www.craterlakelodges.com/careers/
Crawford Caves	volunteers@parks.wa.gov
Crooked Creek Lake	karlee.l.kocon@usace.army.mil
Cross Lake Recreation Area	jason.a.hauser@usace.army.mil
Crystal Cove State Park	john.hunt@parks.ca.gov
Crystal Lake Campground	jpurcell@chartermi.net
Crystal Lake Family Campground	crystallakecamping.com
Crystal River Archaeological State Park	https://volunteers.floridastateparks.org
Crystal River Preserve State Park	https://volunteers.floridastateparks.org
Cuneo Creek Horse Camp	blair.pubols@parks.ca.gov
Curlew Lake State Park	volunteers@parks.wa.gov

Curry Hammock State Park	https://volunteers.floridastateparks.org
Custer State Park Regency Csp Ventures	jobs@custerresorts.com
Cuyamaca Rancho State Park	andrew.ferreira@parks.ca.gov
D.L. Bliss State Park	steven.oriol@parks.ca.gov
Dade Battlefield Historic State Park	https://volunteers.floridastateparks.org
Dagny Johnson Key Largo Hammock Botanical State Park	https://volunteers.floridastateparks.org
Dale Hollow Lake	bradley.potts@usace.army.mil
Dallas Landing Park in Acworth, Georgia	elacher@acworth.org
Dankworth Pond State Park	bworman@azstateparks.gov
Daroga State Park	volunteers@parks.wa.gov
De Leon Springs State Park	https://volunteers.floridastateparks.org
De Queen Lake	victor.r.kuykendall@usace.army.mil
Dead Horse Ranch State Park	bworman@azstateparks.gov
Death Valley Lodging Company	http://www.deathvalleyhotels.com/
Deception Pass State Park	volunteers@parks.wa.gov
Deception Pass State Park-Cornet Bay Fort Casey State Park	volunteers@parks.wa.gov
Deep Creek Tube Center & Campground	www.deepcreekcamping.com

Deep Creek Tube Center Campground	red.bird5@gmail.com
Deer Creek Lake	bonnie.maki@usace.army.mil
Deer Lake State Park	https://volunteers.floridastateparks.org
Degray Lake	jeffrey.s.arthur@usace.army.mil
Delaware Lake	valerie.l.crane@usace.army.mil
Delaware State Parks	dnrec_helpyourpark@state.de.us
Delnor-Wiggins Pass State Park	https://volunteers.floridastateparks.org
Devil's Millhopper Geological State Park	https://volunteers.floridastateparks.org
Dewey Lake	kayla.d.price@usace.army.mil
Diamond M Ranch	www.diamondmranchresort.com/
Diamond Valley Lake	www.dvmarina.com
Dierks Lake/Gillham Lake	trey.a.shelton@usace.army.mil
Dillon Lake	robert.w.cifranic@usace.army.mil
Dimond "O" Campground	www.americanll.com
Dollywood	https://www.dollywood.com/employment
Don Pedro Island State Park	https://volunteers.floridastateparks.org
Dorena Lake	donna.r.bryant@usace.army.mil
Dornan's In The Tetons	https://dornans.com/
Dosewallips State Park	volunteers@parks.wa.gov
Douthat State Park	vspvolunteer@dcr.virginia.gov
Dover Dam	lydia.e.fach@usace.army.mil

Dr. Julian G. Bruce St. George Island State Park	https://volunteers.floridastateparks.org
Drakesbad Guest Ranch	www.drakesbad.com
Driftwood RV Park	http://www.driftwood-rv.com
Dudley Farm Historic State Park	https://volunteers.floridastateparks.org
Dunns Creek State Park	https://volunteers.floridastateparks.org
Dworshak Dam	michelle.b.east@usace.army.mil
East Branch Clarion River Lake	arthur.myers@usace.army.mil
East Brimfield Lake	keith.w.beecher@usace.army.mil
East Lynn Lake	jason.a.kelly@usace.army.mil
Eastman Lake	kenneth.j.myers@usace.army.mil
Eau Galle Lake	william.k.schmidt@usace.army.mil
Econfina River State Park	https://volunteers.floridastateparks.org
Eden Gardens State Park	https://volunteers.floridastateparks.org
Edward Ball Wakulla Springs State Park	https://volunteers.floridastateparks.org
Egmont Key State Park	https://volunteers.floridastateparks.org
El Capitan State Beach	scott.anderson@parks.ca.gov
Eldorado National Forest	www.americanll.com
Ellie Schiller Homosassa Springs State Park	https://volunteers.floridastateparks.org
Emerald Bay State Park	steven.oriol@parks.ca.gov

Emma Wood State Beach	jeffrey.langley@parks.ca.gov
Enid Lake	kyle.c.tedford@usace.army.mil
Estero Bay Preserve State Park	https://volunteers.floridastateparks.org
Eufaula Lake	mark.f.limestall@usace.army.mil
Evangelina Oaks RV Park	evangelineoaksrvpark@gmail.com
Everglades National Park Boat Tours	http://evergladesnationalparkboattoursgulfcoast.com/
Fairy Stone State Park	vspvolunteer@dcr.virginia.gov
Fakahatchee Strand Preserve State Park	https://volunteers.floridastateparks.org
Fall River Lake	jesse.c.busenbarrick@usace.army.mil
Falling Waters State Park	https://volunteers.floridastateparks.org
Falls Lake/B. E. Jordan Lakes	stacee.l.henderson@usace.army.mil
Fanning Springs State Park	https://volunteers.floridastateparks.org
Fashoda Campground	www.americanll.com
Faver-Dykes State Park	https://volunteers.floridastateparks.org
Federation Forest State Park	volunteers@parks.wa.gov
Fern Ridge Lake	donna.r.bryant@usace.army.mil
Fernandina Plaza Historic State Park	https://volunteers.floridastateparks.org
Fields Spring State Park	volunteers@parks.wa.gov
First Landing State Park	vspvolunteer@dcr.virginia.gov
Fishtrap Lake	mark.r.holbrook@usace.army.mil

Flaming Geyser State Park	volunteers@parks.wa.gov
Florida Caverns State Park	https://volunteers.floridastateparks.org
Florida Keys Overseas Heritage State Trail	https://volunteers.floridastateparks.org
Folsom Lake State Recreation Area	flsra.camphost@parks.ca.gov
Fool Hollow Lake Recreation Area	bworman@azstateparks.gov
Forest Capital Museum State Park	https://volunteers.floridastateparks.org
Fort Casey State Park Fort	volunteers@parks.wa.gov
Fort Clinch State Park	https://volunteers.floridastateparks.org
Fort Cooper State Park	https://volunteers.floridastateparks.org
Fort Ebey State Park	volunteers@parks.wa.gov
Fort Flagler Anderson Lake	volunteers@parks.wa.gov
Fort Flagler Historical State Park	bill.drath@parks.wa.gov
Fort Flagler State Park	volunteers@parks.wa.gov
Fort Foster State Historic Site	https://volunteers.floridastateparks.org
Fort George Island Cultural State Park	https://volunteers.floridastateparks.org
Fort Gibson Lake	joshua.w.mathis@usace.army.mil
Fort Martin Scott	fortmartinscott@fbgtx.org
Fort Mose Historic State Park	https://volunteers.floridastateparks.org

Fort Peck Project	susan.e.dalbey@usace.army.mil
Fort Pierce Inlet State Park	https://volunteers.floridastateparks.org
Fort Randall Dam/Lake Francis Case	michael.d.insko@usace.army.mil
Fort Simcoe State Park	volunteers@parks.wa.gov
Fort Stockton RV Park	tammy@fortstocktonrvpark.com
Fort Supply Lake/ Optima Lake	eric.r.summars@usace.army.mil
Fort Townsend State Park	volunteers@parks.wa.gov
Fort Worden State Park	fwv390@parks.wa.gov
Fort Worden State Park	volunteers@parks.wa.gov
Fort Zachary Taylor Historic State Park	https://volunteers.floridastateparks.org
Fountain Of Youth Spa Rv Resort	https://foyspa.com
Franklin Falls/Blackwater Dam	karen.w.hoey@usace.army.mil
Fred Gannon Rocky Bayou State Park	https://volunteers.floridastateparks.org
Frog City Rv Park	rvmanager@lafayettervpark.com
Gainesville To Hawthorne State Trail	https://volunteers.floridastateparks.org
Gamble Rogers Memorial State Recreation Area At Flagler Beach	https://volunteers.floridastateparks.org
Garrison Dam Project/Lake Sakakawea	eric.c.kelsey@usace.army.mil

Gasparilla Island State Park	https://volunteers.floridastateparks.org
Gatewood Park & Reservoir	mmcmanus2000@yahoo.com
Gavins Point Project/Lewis & Clark Lake	karla.j.zentenhors@usace.army.mil
Gaviota State Park	scott.anderson@parks.ca.gov
General James A. Van Fleet State Trail	https://volunteers.floridastateparks.org
George Crady Bridge Fishing Pier State Park	https://volunteers.floridastateparks.org
George W. Andrews Lake	joyce.s.sellers@usace.army.mil
Gerle Creek Campground	www.americanll.com
Gilchrist Blue Springs State Park	https://volunteers.floridastateparks.org
Ginkgo State Park	volunteers@parks.wa.gov
Glacier National Park	www.glacierjobs.com
Glacier National Park	glacierjobs@xanterra.com
Glacier Park Collection By Pursuit	https://www.glacierparkcollection.com/
Glen Echo Resort	tami@glenechoresort.com
Goldendale Observatory State Park	volunteers@parks.wa.gov
Grand Canyon North Rim	http://www.grandcanyonforever.com/
Grand Canyon South Rim	gcjobs@delawarenorth.com
Grand Teton Lodge Company	hr@gtlc.com
Granger Lake	amber.k.owen@usace.army.mil

Grapevine Lake	john.l.mathney@usace.army.mil
Grapevine Lake	john.l.mathney@usace.army.mil
Grayland Beach State Park	volunteers@parks.wa.gov
Grayson Highlands State Park	vspvolunteer@dcr.virginia.gov
Grayson Lake	francis.s.jeffrey@usace.army.mil
Grayton Beach State Park	https://volunteers.floridastateparks.org
Green River Lake	jessica.l.lee@usace.army.mil
Greers Ferry Lake	joseph.d.harper@usace.army.mil
Grenada Lake	gaydon.w.clark@usace.army.mil
Grist Mill State Historic Park	jason.jordon@countyofnapa.org
Grizzly Creek Redwoods State Park	racheal.marte-taylor@parks.ca.gov
Grove River Ranch, Equestrian Center & Retreat	http://groveriverranch.com
Guadalupe Ranger District	dennisbrockman@fs.fed.us
Guard 1 Services	www.gaurd1services.com
Gull Lake Recreation Area	marykay.l.larson@usace.army.mil
Happy Holiday RV Resort	camp@happyholidayrvresort.com
Harlan County Lake	thomas.j.zikmund@usace.army.mil
Harry L. Englebright Lake	tom.bookholtz@usace.army.mil
Hart Ranch Camping Resort	humanresources@hartranchresort.com
Hartwell Lake	thomas.d.bowen@usace.army.mil

Hartwell Lake	thomas.d.bowen@usace.army.mil
Havasu Riviera State Park	bworman@azstateparks.gov
Haw Creek Preserve State Park	https://volunteers.floridastateparks.org
Headwaters Lodge & Cabins at Flagg Ranch	BAEnglish@vailresorts.com
Hearst San Simeon State Park	jared.meichtry@parks.ca.gov
Heartland RV Park	alan@heartlandrvpark.com
Heber Dunes State Vehicle Recreation Area	james.claar@parks.ca.gov
Henderson Beach State Park	https://volunteers.floridastateparks.org
Hendy Woods State Park	alyson.fussell@parks.ca.gov
Hensley Lake/Hidden Dam	nicolas.r.figueroa@usace.army.mil
Heyburn Lake	john.r.hamblen@usace.army.mil
Hickory Hill Camp Resort	service@hickoryhillscamp.com
High Springs Campground	camp@highspringscampground.com
Highland Ridge Campground	eau.galle.lake@usace.army.mil
Highlands Hammock State Park	https://volunteers.floridastateparks.org
Hill RV Resort	info@topofthehillrvresort.com
Hillsborough River State Park	https://volunteers.floridastateparks.org
Hillsdale Lake	james.d.bell@usace.army.mil
Hilton Head Island Motorcoach Resort	manager@hhimr.com
Ho-Hum RV Resort	mhughes47@gmail.com

Holliday Lake State Park-	vspvolunteer@dcr.virginia.gov
Holt Lake/Black Warrior & Tombigbee Lakes	russell.b.barton@usace.army.mil
Homme Lake	christopher.m.botz@usace.army.mil
Homolovi State Park	bworman@azstateparks.gov
Honeymoon Island State Park	https://volunteers.floridastateparks.org
Hontoon Island State Park	https://volunteers.floridastateparks.org
Hoodoo Recreation	www.hoodoo.com
Hoodoo Recreation Services	www.hoodoo.com
Hope Island	volunteers@parks.wa.gov
Hopkinton-Everett Lake	stephen.p.dermody@usace.army.mil
Hopper Bros Christmas Trees	www.hopperbros.com
Hords Creek Lake	brandon.l.moehrle@usace.army.mil
Horseshoe Trails Campground	www.horseshoetrailscamping.com
Hugh Taylor Birch State Park	https://volunteers.floridastateparks.org
Hugo Lake	sarah.m.whorton@usace.army.mil
Humboldt Redwoods State Park	vc@humboldtredwoods.org
Hungry Mother State Park	vspvolunteer@dcr.virginia.gov
Hungry Mountain Ranch	bevhmr@gmail.com
Ichetucknee Springs State Park	https://volunteers.floridastateparks.org

Ichetucknee Trace	https://volunteers.floridastateparks.org
Idaho State Parks	kathryn.hampton@idpr.idaho.gov
Ike Kinswa State Park	volunteers@parks.wa.gov
Illahee State Park	volunteers@parks.wa.gov
Illinois Waterway Farmdale/Fondulac	todd.d.ernenputsch@usace.army.mil
Illinois Waterway Visitor Center	gary.l.shea@usace.army.mil
Imperial Sand Dunes	www.isdpermits.net
Indian Grinding Rock State Historic Park	lee.eal@parks.ca.gov
Indian Key Historic State Park	https://volunteers.floridastateparks.org
Indian River Lagoon Preserve State Park	https://volunteers.floridastateparks.org
Indigo Bluffs RV Park & Resort	visitus@indigobluffs.com
J. Edward Roush Lake	anthony.h.schoenecker@usace.army.mil
J. Percy Priest Lake	carter.robinson@usace.army.mil
Jack Island Preserve	https://volunteers.floridastateparks.org
Jacks Camper Sales	www.jackscampers.com
James River State Park	vspvolunteer@dcr.virginia.gov
Jarrell Cove State Park	volunteers@parks.wa.gov
Jedediah Smith Redwoods State Park	mike.whelan@parks.ca.gov
Jekyll Island Campground	rdouglas@jekyllisland.com
Jennings Randolph Lake	thomas.m.craig@usace.army.mil
Jesse Brent Lower Mississippi River Museum	aaron.w.posner@usace.army.mil

Jim Woodruff Lake & Dam	ruth.c.heying@usace.army.mil
Joe Pool Lake	jeremy.a.spencer@usace.army.mil
Joemma Beach State Park	volunteers@parks.wa.gov
John D. Macarthur Beach State Park	https://volunteers.floridastateparks.org
John Day Lock & Dam/Willow Creek Project	greg.m.volkman@usace.army.mil
John Gorrie Museum State Park	https://volunteers.floridastateparks.org
John H Kerr Dam And Reservoir	david.a.schwartz@usace.army.mil
John Martin Dam	jonathan.b.tague@usace.army.mil
John Paul Hammerschmidt Lake	donnie.l.lindsay@usace.army.mil
John Pennekamp Coral Reef State Park	https://volunteers.floridastateparks.org
John Redmond Lake	gary.a.kepley@usace.army.mil
John U. Lloyd Beach State Park	https://volunteers.floridastateparks.org
John W Flannagan Dam & Reservoir	marty.j.davis@usace.army.mil
Jonathan Dickinson State Park	https://volunteers.floridastateparks.org
Judah P. Benjamin Confederate Memorial At Gamble Plantation Historic State Park	https://volunteers.floridastateparks.org
Kalkaska Campground	kalkaskarvpark@gmail.com

Kampgrounds Enterprises, Inc	http://www.keioutdoor.com/
Kanaskat-Palmer State Park	volunteers@parks.wa.gov
Kanopolis Lake	brock.a.delong@usace.army.mil
Kartchner Caverns State Park	bworman@azstateparks.gov
Katherine Landing At Lake Mohave Marina	www.katherinelanding.com
Kaw Lake	dakota.l.allison@usace.army.mil
Kelly Dahl	www.americanll.com
Kelly Inn Properties, West Yellowstone	westgatemanager@kellyinns.com
Keystone Lake	john.r.hamblen@usace.army.mil or
Kinzua Dam/Allegheny Reservoir	steven.j.lauser@usace.army.mil
Kiptopeke State Park	vspvolunteer@dcr.virginia.gov
Kissimmee Prairie Preserve State Park	https://volunteers.floridastateparks.org
Kitchen Craft Cookware	https://kitchencraftcookware.com/
Kitsap Memorial State Park	volunteers@parks.wa.gov
Klondike RV Park	klondikervpark.com
Knightville Dam and Littleville Lake	matthew.s.coleman@usace.army.mil
Koreshan State Historic Site	https://volunteers.floridastateparks.org
Lac Qui Parle Lake	randy.d.melby@usace.army.mil
Lafayette Blue Springs State Park	https://volunteers.floridastateparks.org

Lake Anna State Park	vspvolunteer@dcr.virginia.gov
Lake Barkley	wesley.r.daveport@usace.army.mil
Lake Chabot	www.lakechabotrecreation.com
Lake Chelan State Park	volunteers@parks.wa.gov
Lake Cumberland	eric.t.matthews@usace.army.mil
Lake Easton State Park	volunteers@parks.wa.gov
Lake Georgetown	bradley.w.arldt@usace.army.mil
Lake Greeson	randy.m.sorrells@usace.army.mil
Lake Gregory Recreation Company	www.lakegregoryrecreation.com
Lake Griffin State Park	https://volunteers.floridastateparks.org
Lake Havasu	lori.field@blackmeadowlanding.com
Lake Havasu State Park	bworman@azstateparks.gov
Lake Hemet	www.lakehemetrecreation.com
Lake Huron	info@huroncountyparks.com
Lake Jackson Mounds Archaeological State Park	https://volunteers.floridastateparks.org
Lake June-In-Winter Scrub State Park	https://volunteers.floridastateparks.org
Lake Kaweah/Terminus Dam	robin.w.lebo@usace.army.mil
Lake Kissimmee State Park	https://volunteers.floridastateparks.org
Lake Louisa State Park	https://volunteers.floridastateparks.org
Lake Manatee State Park	https://volunteers.floridastateparks.org
Lake Mendocino/Coyote Valley Dam	poppy.l.lozoff@usace.army.mil

Lake Nacimiento	www.nacimientoresort.com
Lake O' The Pines/Ferrell's Bridge Dam	robert.l.henderson@usace.army.mil
Lake Oahe & Dam/Beaver Creek	john.f.voeller@usace.army.mil
Lake Oahe And Dam	phillip.r.sheffield@usace.army.mil
Lake Okeechobee Waterway	robert.r.hill@usace.army.mil
Lake Oroville State Recreation Area	christopher.beehner@parks.ca.gov
Lake Osprey Rv Resort	www.robertresorts.com
Lake Osprey RV Resort	lakeosprey@robertsresorts.com
Lake Red Rock	mark.r.pollastrini@usace.army.mil
Lake Sacajawea / Ice Harbor Lock & Dam	heather.l.geertsen@usace.army.mil
Lake Sammamish State Park	volunteers@parks.wa.gov
Lake San Antonio	www.lakesanantonioresort.com
Lake Sharpe/Big Bend Project	robert.l.karlen@usace.army.mil
Lake Shelbyville	ashley.s.florey@usace.army.mil
Lake Sidney Lanier	daniel.l.brownlow@usace.army.mil
Lake Sonoma	emily.t.kohl@usace.army.mil
Lake State Park	volunteers@parks.wa.gov
Lake Sylvia State Park	volunteers@parks.wa.gov
Lake Talquin State Park	https://volunteers.floridastateparks.org
Lake Texoma	tanner.l.mcadams@usace.army.mil

Lake Washington Ship Canal/Hiram M. Chittenden Locks	kathryn.f.mcgillvray@usace.army.mil
Lake Wenatchee State Park	volunteers@parks.wa.gov
Lake Wood Park	mhenneke@gbra.org
Lakes/Dry Falls Visitor Center	volunteers@parks.wa.gov
Lakeside Camp Park	lakesiecamppark@charter.net
Lakewood RV Resort	info@lakewoodrvresort.com
Larrabee State Park	volunteers@parks.wa.gov
Lassen Café & Gift, Lassen Volcanic National Park	www.lassenrecreation.com
Laurel River Lake	robert.r.hill@usace.army.mil
Lavon Lake	jonathan.e.boyce@usace.army.mil
Lavon Lake	jonathan.e.boyce@usace.army.mil
Leaf Verde RR Resort	http://www.leafverde.com
Leech Lake	gus.garbe@usace.army.mil
Leesville Lake	lydia.e.fach@usace.army.mil
Leisure Resort	http://www.leisurecamp.net
Leo Carillo State Park	lee.hawkins@parks.ca.gov
Letchworth-Love Mounds Archaeological State Park	https://volunteers.floridastateparks.org
Lewis And Clark State Park	volunteers@parks.wa.gov
Lewis And Clark Trail State Park	volunteers@parks.wa.gov
Lewisville Lake/Ray Roberts Lake	james.m.stegall@usace.army.mil

Libby Dam/Lake Koocanusa	susan.j.james@usace.army.mil
LIGHTNER CREEK CAMPGROUND.	llcampground@gmail.com
Lignumvitae Key Botanical State Park	https://volunteers.floridastateparks.org
Lime Kiln State Park	volunteers@parks.wa.gov
Lincoln National Forest Guadalupe District	kelsey.Smith2@usda.gov
Lincoln Rock State Park	volunteers@parks.wa.gov
Little Basin Group Campground	www.littlebasin.org
Little Lake	www.lakehemetrecreation.com/littlelake
Little Manatee River State Park	https://volunteers.floridastateparks.org
Little Rock District Office	chris.l.smith@usace.army.mil
Little Talbot Island State Park	https://volunteers.floridastateparks.org
Long Branch Lake	michael.p.kuntz@usace.army.mil
Long Key State Park	https://volunteers.floridastateparks.org
Long Lake Trailhead	www.americanll.com
Lookout Point Lake	donna.r.bryant@usace.army.mil
Loon Lake Campground	www.americanll.com
Los Vaqueros Watershed	www.norcalfishing.com/los_vaqueros
Lost Creek Lake	anthony.j.johnson@usace.army.mil
Lost Creek Lake	dll-cenwp-rogue-rangers@usace.army.mil
Lost Dutchman State Park	bworman@azstateparks.gov

Louisville District Office	clifton.r.kilpatrick@usace.army.mil
Lovers Key State Park	https://volunteers.floridastateparks.org
Lower Granite Lock & Dam Natural Resource Office/Lower Granite Lake	dawn.waldal@usace.army.mil
Lower Wekiva River Preserve State Park	https://volunteers.floridastateparks.org
Loyalhanna Lake	ben.a.caparelli@usace.army.mil
Loyalhanna Lake Recreation	ben.a.caparelli@usace.army.mil
Lt. Blender Cocktails	http://ltblender.com
Lucky Peak Lake & Dam	keith.b.hyde@usace.army.mil
Lyman Lake State Park	bworman@azstateparks.gov
Lyons Ferry	volunteers@parks.wa.gov
Mackerricher State Park	alyson.fussell@parks.ca.gov
Madira Bickel Mound State Archaeological Site	https://volunteers.floridastateparks.org
Madison Blue Spring State Park	https://volunteers.floridastateparks.org
Mahoning Creek Lake	grover.m.pegg@usace.army.mil
Malakof Diggins State Historic Park-	brooke.betz@parks.ca.gov
Malibu Creek State Park	lee.hawkins@parks.ca.gov
Manatee Springs State Park	https://volunteers.floridastateparks.org
Manchester State Park	alyson.fussell@parks.ca.gov
Manchester State Park	volunteers@parks.wa.gov
Manresa State Beach	arlene.shaffer@parks.ca.gov

Mansfield Hollow Lake	michelle.l.cucchi@usace.army.mil
Manzanita Lake Camper Service Store	www.lassenrecreation.com
Maple Grove Koa	https://koa.com/campgrounds/minneapolis-northwest/
Marion Reservoir	scott.a.mccrone@usace.army.mil
Marjorie Harris Carr Cross Florida Greenway	https://volunteers.floridastateparks.org
Marjorie Kinnan Rawlings Historic State Park	https://volunteers.floridastateparks.org
Martins Fork Lake	david.c.robinson@usace.army.mil
Martis Creek Lake	jason.c.worden@usace.army.mil
Maryhill State Park	volunteers@parks.wa.gov
Mcfarland State Historic Park	bworman@azstateparks.gov
Mcgrath State Beach	jeffrey.langley@parks.ca.gov
Mcnary Lock & Dam/Lake Wallula	david.f.mcdermott@usace.army.mil
Meeker Park Campground	www.americanll.com
Melvern Lake	buck.a.walker@usace.army.mil
Mendocino Headlands State Park	fordhouse@mcn.org
Michael J. Kirwan Dam	julie.r.stone@usace.army.mil
Midwest Outdoor Resorts	sued@stcroixriverresort.com
Mike Roess Gold Head Branch State Park	https://volunteers.floridastateparks.org
Milford Lake	blake.d.mcpherren@usace.army.mil

Mill Creek Dam/Bennington Lake	cady.l.tyron@usace.army.mil
Millersylvania State Park	volunteers@parks.wa.gov
Millerton Lake State Recreation Area	www.parks.ca.gov/millertonlake
Millwood Lake	brooke.s.kervin@usace.army.mil
Mississinewa Lake	gregory.n.carpenter@usace.army.mil
Mississippi River Project Pool	bret.r.streckwald@usace.army.mil
Mississippi River Project Pool:Shady Creek Recreation Area	jacob.j.kresel@usace.army.mil
Mitchell Lake Trailhead	www.americanll.com
Moab Valley RV Resort	rshort@suncommunities.com
Mobile District Office	consuela.a.gunter@usace.army.mil
Mohawk Dam/North Branch Kokosing	bryan.r.muroski@usace.army.mil
Mohicanville Dam	bryan.r.muroski@usace.army.mil
Monroe Lake	gary.j.staigl@usace.army.mil
Monroe Navigation Project	diane.golden@usace.army.mil
Montana De Oro State Park	jennifer.wilson@parks.ca.gov
Monterey County Parks	www.co.monterey.ca.us/parks
Moose Hillock Camping Resort in Lake George,	sbparadis@moosehillock.com
Moran State Park	volunteers@parks.wa.gov
Morro Bay State Park	jennifer.wilson@parks.ca.gov
Mosquito Creek Lake	kathryn.fatula@usace.army.mil

Mound Key Archaeological State Park	https://volunteers.floridastateparks.org
Mount Morris Dam	juliana.e.smith@usace.army.mil
Mount Rushmore Resort And Lodge At Palmer Gulch	http://www.palmergulch.com/
Mountain Ridge Cabins and Lodging	www.mountainridgemotel.com/employment
Mt St Helens Visitors Center	volunteers@parks.wa.gov
Mt St Helens Visitors Center	volunteers@parks.wa.gov
Mud Mountain Dam	laura.g.robinson@usace.army.mil
Myakka River State Park	https://volunteers.floridastateparks.org
Myrtle Beach State Park – Nature Center	https://southcarolinaparks.com/myrtle-beach
Mystery Bay State Park	fwv390@parks.wa.gov
Mystery Bay-Fort Flagler	volunteers@parks.wa.gov
National Great Rivers Museum	janet.k.meredith@usace.army.mil
Natural Bridge Battlefield Historic State Park	https://volunteers.floridastateparks.org
Natural Bridge State Park	vspvolunteer@dcr.virginia.gov
Natural Tunnel State Park	vspvolunteer@dcr.virginia.gov
Nature Coast State Trail	https://volunteers.floridastateparks.org
Naugatuck River Basin	marissa.l.wright@usace.army.mil
Navarro Mills Lake	teresa.j.ezersky@usace.army.mil
Nevada RV Park	desertroserv@aol.com

New Hogan Lake	allen.a.aguas@usace.army.mil
Newt Graham Lock & Dam	joshua.w.mathis@usace.army.mil
Next Day Funding	www.nextdayfunders.com
Nimrod Lake	lisa.a.owens@usace.army.mil
Nolin River Lake	jon.p.fillingham@usace.army.mil
Nolte State Park	volunteers@parks.wa.gov
Nolte State Park	volunteers@parks.wa.gov
Norfork Lakes & Bull Shoals	kevin.patterson@usace.army.mil
North Fork Of The Pound River	marty.j.davis@usace.army.mil
North Hartland Lake	heather.l.morse@usace.army.mil
North Lake Rv Park And Campground	http://www.northlakervparkandcampground.com
North Park	manager@moosecreekcafe.net
North Peninsula State Park	https://volunteers.floridastateparks.org
O'leno State Park	https://volunteers.floridastateparks.org
Oakwood RV Park	oakwoodrv@yahoo.com
Ocala North RV Park	http://www.ocalanorthrv.com/
Occoneechee State Park	vspvolunteer@dcr.virginia.gov
Ocean City State Park	volunteers@parks.wa.gov
Ocean Waves Campground	www.oceanwavescampground.com
Ochlockonee River State Park	https://volunteers.floridastateparks.org
Okatibbee Lake	nikia.r.angevine@usace.army.mil

Okeechobee Battlefield Historic State Park	https://volunteers.floridastateparks.org
Okefenokee Swamp Park	bell@atc.cc
Olallie State Park	volunteers@parks.wa.gov
Old Hickory Lake	dylon.j.anderson@usace.army.mil
Old River Control Project	clyde.j.harvey@usace.army.mil
Oleta River State Park	https://volunteers.floridastateparks.org
Olive Ridge	www.americanll.com
Olustee Battlefield Historic State Park	https://volunteers.floridastateparks.org
Omaha District Office	harold.m.key@usace.army.mil
Oologah Lake	jason.a.person@usace.army.mil
Orman House Historic State Park	https://volunteers.floridastateparks.org
Orwell Lake	randy.d.melby@usace.army.mil
Osage Beach RV Park	info@osagebeachrvpark.net
Oscar Scherer State Park	https://volunteers.floridastateparks.org
Otter Brook/Surry Mountain Lakes	christie.l.baker@usace.army.mil
Ouachita Lake	amy.j.shultz@usace.army.mil
Ouray RV Park	ourayrvpark@gmail.com
Ozark Lake	donnie.ll.lindsay@usace.army.mil
Pacific Beach State Park	volunteers@parks.wa.gov
Paint Creek Lake	connor.s.santee@usace.army.mil
Paintsville Lake	nathan.a.shelton@usace.army.mil
Palatka-To-Lake Butler State Trail	https://volunteers.floridastateparks.org

Palatka-To-St. Augustine State Trail	https://volunteers.floridastateparks.org
Palm Springs/Joshua Tree Koa	www.keioutdoorjobs.com
Palm View Gardens RVResort	https://www.rvresorts.com/palm-view-gardens.html
Palomar Mountain State Park	jessica.murany@parks.ca.gov
Paradise Point State Park	volunteers@parks.wa.gov
Pat Mayse Lake	sarah.k.noel@usace.army.mil
Patagonia Lake State Park	bworman@azstateparks.gov
Patapsco Valley State Park	zachary.bruce@maryland.gov
Patoka Lake	john.l.hovis@usace.army.mil
Patrick's Point State Park	maury.morningstar@parks.ca.gov
Paul Nelson Farm	lindsay@paulnelsonfarm.com
Pawnee Campground	www.americanll.com
Paynes Creek Historic State Park	https://volunteers.floridastateparks.org
Paynes Prairie Preserve State Park	https://volunteers.floridastateparks.org
Peace Arch State Park	volunteers@parks.wa.gov
Peaceful Valley Campground	www.americanll.com
Pearson-Skubitz Big Hill Lake	barbara.j.busenbarrick@usace.army.mil
Penrose Point State Park	volunteers@parks.wa.gov

Perdido Key State Park	https://volunteers.floridastateparks.org
Perry Lake	wesley.j.henson@usace.army.mil
Pfeiffer Big Sur State Park	sharon.pieniak@parks.ca.gov
Philadelphia District Office	nathan.t.freiwald@usace.army.mil
Philpott Lake	richard.a.wigley@usace.army.mil
Picacho Peak State Park	bworman@azstateparks.gov
Pine Creek Lake	corey.claborn@usace.army.mil
Pine Flat Lake	www.lrn.usace.army.mil/volunteer/
Pine Flat Lake & Dam	isac.g.hermosilla@usace.army.mil
Pioneer River Resort	pioneerrr@sbcglobal.net
Pipestem Lake	robert.j.martin@usace.army.mil
Pismo State Beach	jorge.barajas-ochoa@parks.ca.gov
Place Golf Course and RV Resort	info@likelyplace.com
Pleasant Hill Lake	bryan.r.muroski@usace.army.mil
Plumas-Eureka State Park	scott.elliott@parks.ca.gov
Pocahontas State Park	vspvolunteer@dcr.virginia.gov
Point Mugu State Park	lee.hawkins@parks.ca.gov
Pokegama Lake & Dam/Winnie Dam	jeff.j.cook@usace.army.mil
Poland Spring Campground	jobs@polandspringcamp.com
Polson RV Park	carlisa@polsonrvresort.com
Pomme De Terre Lake	devin.t.holt@usace.army.mil
Pomona Lake	william.k.bolt@usace.army.mil
Ponce De Leon Springs State Park	https://volunteers.floridastateparks.org

Ponderosa Cove	www.americanll.com
Portola Redwoods State Park	tyler.knapp@parks.ca.gov
Potholes State Park	volunteers@parks.wa.gov
Potlatch State Park	volunteers@parks.wa.gov
Powhatan State Park -	vspvolunteer@dcr.virginia.gov
Prairie Creek Redwoods State Park	leslie.reyes@parks.ca.gov
Premium RV Resorts, Lincoln City	lincolncitymanager@premierrvresorts.com
Price's Scrub	https://volunteers.floridastateparks.org
Prince William Forest RV Campground	bob.junker@racpack.com
Proctor Lake	stephanie.a.jones@usace.army.mil
Proctor Lake, TX	www.usace.army.mil/Missions/CivilWorks/Recreation/VolunteerClearinghouse.aspx
Proctor Landing Park in Acworth, Georgia	elacher@acworth.org
Pumpkin Hill Creek Preserve State Park	https://volunteers.floridastateparks.org
Quagga Inspection Services, Llc	www.quaggainspections.com
R.D. Bailey Lake	johnathan.a.browning@usace.army.mil
Rainbow Falls State Park Rasar State Park	volunteers@parks.wa.gov
Rainbow Lakes Campground	www.americanll.com
Rainbow Springs State Park	https://volunteers.floridastateparks.org
Rainier Guest Services	http://mtrainierguestservices.com/about-us/careers/
Ramona Oaks RV Resort	manager@rorvpark.com

Rathbun Lake	john.p.pasa@usace.army.mil
Ravine Gardens State Park	https://volunteers.floridastateparks.org
Raystown Lake	alicia.e.wicker@usace.army.mil
Red Gate RV Park	theredgaterv@gmail.com
Red Rock Lake	mark.r.pollastrini@usace.army.mil
Red Rock State Park	bworman@azstateparks.gov
Refugio State Beach	scott.anderson@parks.ca.gov
Rend Lake	cassie.l.magsig@usace.army.mil
Reynolds Resorts in Northern California	julie@reynoldsresorts.com
Richard B. Russell Dam & Lake	zachary.e.baldwin@usace.army.mil
Richardson Grove State Park	vc@humboldtredwoods.org
Rio Verde RV Park	nfo@rioverdervpark
Riordan Mansion State Historic Park	bworman@azstateparks.gov
River Island State Park	bworman@azstateparks.gov
River Rise Preserve State Park	https://volunteers.floridastateparks.org
River's Edge RV Campground	nburmester@ufl.edu
Riverbank, CA Seasonal Park	sfitzpatrick@riverbank.org
Rivers Project Office	angela.smith@usace.army.mil
Riverside State Park	volunteers@parks.wa.gov
Rock Shadows RV Resort	http://www.rockshadows.com
Rock Shadows RV Resort in Apache Junction	rockshadowsrv@hotmail.com

Rock Springs Run State Reserve	https://volunteers.floridastateparks.org
Rockin' River Ranch State Park	bworman@azstateparks.gov
Rockport State Park	volunteers@parks.wa.gov
Rogue River Basin Project	joyce.a.szalwinsii@usace.army.mil
Roman Nose State Park	kyle.bernis@travelok.com
Roman Nose State Park	kyle.bernis@travelok.com
Roper Lake State Park	bworman@azstateparks.gov
Rough River Lake	adam.d.taylor@usace.army.mil
Rum River Campground RV Park	dianejs747@gmail.com
Rush No More Campground	info@rushnomore.com
Russellville Project: Dardanelle Lake	scott.j.fryer@usace.army.mil
Russian Gulch State Park	alyson.fussell@parks.ca.gov
RV Transport Inc	www.rvtransport.com
Sacajawea State Park	volunteers@parks.wa.gov
Saco River Camping Area	jobs@sacorivercampingarea.com
Sacramento District Office	alicia.s.unsinn@usace.army.mil
Saddleback Butte State Park	kevin.overduin@parks.ca.gov
Saint Paul District Office	tamryn.johnson@usace.army.mil
Salamonie Lake	john.d.scheiber@usace.army.mil
Salt Point State Park	trevor.nealy@parks.ca.gov

Salton Sea SRA	salton.sea@parks.ca.gov
Saltwater State Park	volunteers@parks.wa.gov
Sam Rayburn Reservoir	cody.l.turner@usace.army.mil
San Diego County Parks	www.sdparks.org
San Diego Parks	cheryl.wegner@sdcounty.ca.gov
San Felasco Hammock Preserve State Park	https://volunteers.floridastateparks.org
San Francisco Bay Model Visitor Center	joanne.jarvis@usace.army.mil
San Francisco District Office-Nrs Office/Warm Springs Dam	charles.fenwick@usace.army.mil
San Marcos De Apalache Historic State Park	https://volunteers.floridastateparks.org
San Pedro Underwater Archaeological Preserve State Park	https://volunteers.floridastateparks.org
San Rafael State Natural Area	bworman@azstateparks.gov
San Simeon Campground	jared.meichtry@parks.ca.gov
Sand Flat Campground	www.americanll.com
Sandy Lake & Dam	courtney.m.kinnett@usace.army.mil
Santa Rosa Lake	paul.d.sanchez@usace.army.mil
Sardis Lake	chris.r.gurner@usace.army.mil
Sardis Lake	shae.harrison@usace.army.mil
Savannah District Office	ryan.d.hartwig@usace.army.mil
Savannah District Office	joseph.w.melton@usace.army.mil

Savannas Preserve State Park	https://volunteers.floridastateparks.org
Saylorville Lake	emma.m.nelson@usace.army.mil
Scenic Beach State Park	volunteers@parks.wa.gov
Scenic Canyons Recreational Services	www.sceniccanyons.com
Schafer State Park	volunteers@parks.wa.gov
Schulenburg RV Park	www.schulenburgrvpark.com
Sea Rocks RV Cove	www.sealrocksrv.com
Seabranch Preserve State Park	https://volunteers.floridastateparks.org
Seaquest State Park	volunteers@parks.wa.gov
Seattle District Office	taylor.m.johnson@usace.army.mil
Sebastian Inlet State Park	https://volunteers.floridastateparks.org
Sequim Bay (Ramblewood)	volunteers@parks.wa.gov
Sequim Bay State Park	volunteers@parks.wa.gov
Shasta Recreation Company	www.shastatrinitycamping.com
Shelter Cove Resort & Marina	jput@highwaywestvacations.com
Shenandoah River State Park	vspvolunteer@dcr.virginia.gov
Shenango Lake	matthew.pook@usace.army.mil
Shenango River Lake	jason.cote@usace.army.mil
Shipcreek RV Park	shipcreek@bestofalaskatravel.com
Shipshewana Campground	shipshewanacampgroundnorth@yahoo.com
Signal Mountain Lodge	http://www.workatsignal.com/
Silver Falls Lodge & Conference Center	www.silverfallslodge.com

Silver Fork Campground	www.americanll.com
Silver Springs State Park	https://volunteers.floridastateparks.org
Skagway RV Park	cmeier@bestofalaskatravel.com
Skiatook Lake	jeff.walker@usace.army.mil
Sky Valley Resorts	www.skyvalleyresorts.com
Sky Valley/Caliente Resorts	anasha.berry@skyvalleyresorts.com
Skyline Ranch Rv Park	http://www.skylineranchrvpark.com
Skyway Camping Resort	skywaycamping@gmail.com
Skyway Fishing Pier State Park	https://volunteers.floridastateparks.org
Smith Mountain Lake State Park	vspvolunteer@dcr.virginia.gov
Smithville Lake	jaime.d.picken@usace.army.mil
Smithwoods RV Park	deblennen@aol.com
Somerville Lake	jennifer.r.schultz.plair@usace.army.mil
Sonoita Creek State Natural Area	bworman@azstateparks.gov
South Dakota State Parks	www.gfp.sd.gov
Southeast Publications	www.southeastpublications.com
Southern Cross	www.southerncrossinc.com
Southfork State Park	https://volunteers.floridastateparks.org
Spencer Spit State Park	volunteers@parks.wa.gov
Splash Landing Waterpark	waterpark@marktwainlanding.com
Spook Cave and Campgrouond	spookcave@spookcave.com

Sportsman's Campground & Mountain Cabins	jonreed@sportsmanscampground.com
Spring Creek Campground & Trout Ranch	springcreekcampground@yahoo.com
Spruce Lake Rv Resort	https://sprucelakerv.com/
Square Lake State Park	volunteers@parks.wa.gov
Squilchuck State Park	volunteers@parks.wa.gov
St. Andrews State Park	https://volunteers.floridastateparks.org
St. Louis District Office	jonathan.w.schulte@usace.army.mil
St. Lucie Inlet Preserve State Park	https://volunteers.floridastateparks.org
St. Marks River State Park	https://volunteers.floridastateparks.org
St. Sebastian River Preserve State Park	https://volunteers.floridastateparks.org
Stanislaus National Forest	www.americanll.com
Stanislaus River Parks	hilary.a.coleman@usace.army.mil
Stanislaus River Parks	
State Park Olmstead State Park	volunteers@parks.wa.gov
Staunton River State Park	vspvolunteer@dcr.virginia.gov
Steamboat Rock State Park	volunteers@parks.wa.gov
Stephen Foster Folk Culture Center State Park	https://volunteers.floridastateparks.org
Stockton Lake	derrick.s.phillips@usace.army.mil
Stoneridge RV Park & Resort	rvparkusa@gmail.com

Stonewall Jackson Lake	christopher.s.hannah@usace.army.mil
Stony Brook Recreation And Camping	www.stonybrookrec.com
Strates Shows, Inc. Carnivals	www.strates.com
Stump Pass Beach State Park	https://volunteers.floridastateparks.org
Stumpy Meadows Campground	www.americanll.com
Success Lake	robert.moreno@usace.army.mil
Sucia Island State Park	volunteers@parks.wa.gov
Sucia Island State Park	volunteers@parks.wa.gov
Sugar Barge Resort & Marina	www.sugarbarge.com
Sugar Barge RV Resort & Marina	sugarbargetracy@comcast.net
Sugar Pine Point State Park	steven.oriol@parks.ca.gov
Summersville Lake	michael.l.mccoy@usace.army.mil
Sun Lakes/Dry Falls State Park	volunteers@parks.wa.gov
Sunrise Campgrounds	
Sunset Campground	www.americanll.com
Susitna Salmon Cente	arri@arrialaska.org
Sutton Lake	keith.a.nuckles@usace.army.mil
Suwannee River State Park	https://volunteers.floridastateparks.org
Suwannee River Wilderness Trail	https://volunteers.floridastateparks.org
Sweetwater Campground	www.americanll.com

Sweetwater River Ranch	sweetwaterriverranch@gmail.com
Sycamore Lodge	rrjones@travelresorts.com
T. H. Stone Memorial St. Joseph Peninsula State Park	https://volunteers.floridastateparks.org
Table Rock Lake	emily.t.wooldridge@usace.army.mil
Talbot Islands Geopark	https://volunteers.floridastateparks.org
Talkeetna Alaskan Lodge	http://www.alaskacollection.com/corporate/careers/
Tall Texan Campground	janusztylicki344@gmail.com
Tallahassee-St. Marks Geo Park	https://volunteers.floridastateparks.org
Tallahassee-St. Marks Historic Railroad State Trail	https://volunteers.floridastateparks.org
Tarkiln Bayou Preserve State Park	https://volunteers.floridastateparks.org
Taylorsville Lake	evan.s.mckinney@usace.army.mil
Tenkiller Ferry Lake/Webbers Falls Pool	brent.c.buford@usace.army.mil
Tennessee Tombigbee Waterway-Bay Springs	steven.c.koon@usace.army.mil
Tennessee Tombigbee-Aberdeen/Columbus	adam.r.prentice@usace.army.mil
Tennessee-Tombigbee Waterway/Tom Bevill Visitor Center	adam.r.prentice@usace.army.mil
Terra Ceia Preserve State Park	https://volunteers.floridastateparks.org
Texas Freedom RV Village	manager@texasfreedomrvvillage.com
Texas Trails Rv Resort	www.texastrailsrv.com

The Barnacle Historic State Park	https://volunteers.floridastateparks.org
The California Parks Company	www.calparksco.com
The Dalles Lock & Dam/Lake Celilo	amber.c.tilton@usace.army.mil
The Lemon Cove Village RV Park	http://lemoncovevillagervpark.com
The Lodges Of The Northern Big Horn Mountains	http://lodgesofthenorthernbighornmountains.com/
The Ranch At Little Hills	www.littlehillsweddings.com
The Virginian RV Park in Jackson Hole	virginianrv@gmail.com
Theodore Roosevelt Medora Foundation	http://www.medora.com/employment/
Three Rivers State Park	https://volunteers.floridastateparks.org
Timber Ridge in Mountain Lakes Resort	timerridgepoa@yahoo.com
Time Keepers Security Mgt.	info@tieronegroup.com
Tioga-Hammond & Cowanesque Lake	molly.a.wilson@usace.army.mil
Tionesta Lake	jason.a.bowers@usace.army.mil
Toad Suck Ferry L/D/Maumelle Park	thomas.ryan.king@usace.army.mil
Tom Jenkins Dam	robert.w.cifranic@usace.army.mil
Tomoka State Park	https://volunteers.floridastateparks.org
Top Of The Hill RV Resort	www.topofthehillrvresort.com
Topsail Hill Preserve State Park	https://volunteers.floridastateparks.org

Torreya State Park	https://volunteers.floridastateparks.org
Town Bluff Dam/B.A.Steinhagen Lake	cody.l.turner@usace.army.mil
Travelers Campground	dreamcamper@juno.com
Tri-Lakes	timothy.a.rose@usace.army.mil
Tropic Island Resort	manager@tropicislandresort.com
Troy Spring State Park	https://volunteers.floridastateparks.org
Tully Lake	jeffrey.c.mangum@usace.army.mil
Tulsa District Office	jason.m.knight@usace.army.mil
Turlock SRA	www.americanll.com
Tuttle Creek Lake	angelia.j.lentz@usace.army.mil
Twanoh State Park	volunteers@parks.wa.gov
Twenty-Five Mile Creek State Park	volunteers@parks.wa.gov
Twin Harbors State Park	volunteers@parks.wa.gov
Two Rivers Landing RV Resort	info@tworiversrvresort.com
Tygart Lake	stacy.e.lewis@usace.army.mil
UPC Gate Services	www.upcgate.com
Upper Mississippi River Pool #1-10	randall.r.urich@usace.army.mil
USACE Volunteers	www.corpslakes.us/volunteer
USI RV Park	usirvpark.com
Vail Lake Resort	www.vaillakeresort.com
Valley View Christmas Trees	www.valleyviewchristmastrees.org
Van Horn Texas RV Park	http://www.vanhorntexasrvpark.com

Vandamme State Park	alyson.fussell@parks.ca.gov
Ventures West Inc.	http://www.ventureswestinc.com/
Verde River Greenway State Natural Area	bworman@azstateparks.gov
Verde Valley Archaeology Center	https://www.verdevalleyarchaeology.org
Vern Whitaker Horse Camp	norbert.ruhmke@parks.ca.gov
Vicksburg District Office	jonathan.d.harrell@usace.army.mil
Vista Resorts	marshelew@vistaresorts.net
W. Kerr Scott Dam & Reservoir	johnny.e.jones@usace.army.mil
Waccasassa Bay Preserve State Park	https://volunteers.floridastateparks.org
Waco Lake	michael.j.champagne@usace.army.mil
Wales West Rv Resort	www.waleswest.com
Wall Drug	http://www.walldrug.com/about-us/employment
Walla Walla District Office	michael.j.swenson@usace.army.mil
Wallace Falls State Park	volunteers@parks.wa.gov
Wallowa Lake Tramway	www.wallowalaketramway.com
Walter F. George Lake	william.a.hancock@usace.army.mil
Wanapum State Park	volunteers@parks.wa.gov
Wappapello Lake Management	rachel.r.lemons@usace.army.mil
Washington Oaks Gardens State Park	https://volunteers.floridastateparks.org

Wassamki Springs Campground	www.wassamkisprings.com
Waurika Lake Office	luke.t.prichard@usace.army.mil
Weeki Wachee Springs State Park	https://volunteers.floridastateparks.org
Wekiwa Springs State Park	https://volunteers.floridastateparks.org
Wellington Camping Park	www.wellingtoncampingparkleenh.com
Wenatchee Confluence State Park	volunteers@parks.wa.gov
Wench Creek Campground	www.americanll.com
Werner-Boyce Salt Springs State Park	https://volunteers.floridastateparks.org
Wes Skiles Peacock Springs State Park	https://volunteers.floridastateparks.org
West Fork Lake	stephanie.a.ison@usace.army.mil
West Hill Dam/Charles River	viola.m.bramel@usace.army.mil
West Point Lake	steven.m.rector@usace.army.mil
West Thompson Lake	michelle.l.cucchi@usace.army.mil
Westmoreland State Park	vspvolunteer@dcr.virginia.gov
Westport Union-Landing State Beach	alyson.fussell@parks.ca.gov
Westville Lake	keith.w.beecher@usace.army.mil
White River RV Park & Campground	jojimwrc@aol.com
Whitney Lake Project Office/Aquilla Dam & Lake	jarod.d.briscoe@usace.army.mil

Wild Horse Project	http://wildhorseproject.org
Wildwood Campground & RV Park	ryan@wildwoodcamping.com
William H Harsha Lake	samantha.k.bachelder@usace.army.mil
Wilson Lake	zach.d.hlad@usace.army.mil
Windley Key Fossil Reef Geological State Park	https://volunteers.floridastateparks.org
Wingate Creek State Park	https://volunteers.floridastateparks.org
Withlacoochee State Trail	https://volunteers.floridastateparks.org
Wolf Creek Campground	www.americanll.com
Wolf Creek National Fish Hatchery	https://www.fws.gov/wolfcreek
Woodcock Creek Lake & Union City Dam	joseph.d.arnett@usace.army.mil
Woodruff Lake	myers.hawkins@usace.army.mil
Woodson Bridge SRA	www.americanll.com
Wright Patman Lake	james.m.bransford@usace.army.mil
Xanterra Travel Collection	https://www.xanterra.com/who-we-are/careers/
Yakima Sportsman State Park	volunteers@parks.wa.gov
Yatesville Lake	andrew.j.auxier@usace.army.mil
Ybor City Museum State Park	https://volunteers.floridastateparks.org
Yellow Bluff Fort Historic State Park	https://volunteers.floridastateparks.org
Yellow River Marsh Preserve State Park	https://volunteers.floridastateparks.org

Yellowjacket Campground	www.americanll.com
Yellowstone Forever	www.yellowstone.org
Yellowstone General Stores	ygsjobs@delawarenorth.com
Yellowstone Golf Resort	http://www.yellowstonegolfresort.com
Yellowstone Grizzly RV Park and Cabin	www.ventureswestinc.com
Yellowstone National Park Lodges	http://www.yellowstonejobs.com/
Yellowstone Park Service Stations Inc.	http://ypss.com/
Yellowstone Vacations	https://www.yellowstonevacations.com/jobs/west-yellowstone-jobs
YMCA Of The Rockies	http://workintherockies.org/
Yogi in the Smokies	camp@jellystonecherokee.com
Yosemite RV Resort	yosemite@rvcoutdoors.com
Youghiogheny River Lake	vincent.klinkner@usace.army.mil
Yulee Sugar Mill Ruins Historic State Park	https://volunteers.floridastateparks.org
Yuma Quartermaster Depot State Historic Park	bworman@azstateparks.gov
Yuma Territorial Prison State Historic Park	bworman@azstateparks.gov
Zion Mountain Ranch	careers@zmr.com

SECTION 4

ADDITIONAL RESOURCES

Common Interview Questions

Questions to Ask Employers

Websites for Job Listings

Sample Work Agreement

RV Glossary

COMMON INTERVIEW QUESTIONS

After you've submitted your resume, filled out the application and have confirmed your interview date- it's time to prepare! Interviews can be intimidating especially if you really want the job and need to be in the location during a specific time.

Take some time before jumping online or on the phone with the employer to brush up on your interviewing skills! Make sure you can easily and confidently answer these basic interview questions and you'll be a step ahead the rest!

- How did you hear about this position?
- Describe yourself in 3 words.
- Why should we hire you?
- What makes you a good fit for this position?
- Why are you interested in working for us?
- What are your strengths?
- What are your greatest weaknesses?
- Name three things you would like to improve on?
- Are you willing to work holidays/weekends?
- Is your availability open/flexible during our peak season?
- Do you have any vacations or trips planned during your time here?
- Are you able to commit to the entire season?
- What are your salary requirements?
- Are you willing to work 40+ hours a week?
- Are you a leader or a follower?
- Are you comfortable helping out in other departments?
- Tell me about your customer service skill?
- What experience do you have in campground jobs?
- What would your most recent supervisor say about you?
- Tell me about an accomplishment you are most proud of.
- Tell me about a time you made a mistake and how you fixed it.
- Tell me about a time you handled a difficult situation and the outcome.

- Tell me about a time you had to deal with an angry or irate customer?
- How do you handle pressure?
- Do you work better independently or as a team?
- Explain the gap in your employment between these two dates?
- What questions do you have for me?

QUESTIONS FOR EMPLOYERS

At some point in the interview or maybe in your email communications with employers you wish to work for, you'll need to make sure you have the answers to pertinent questions like the ones listed below.

Knowing exactly what you're getting yourself into and getting the most details you can about each job, is imperative. You'll need this information to make the best decisions and to compare each position against others that may seem similar on the surface.

The questions I've detailed below are just the start of what you might need to know. To be perfectly honest, it all depends on what position you're applying to, who you're working for and what has already been discussed. Use these questions as a guide and ask them in the order that makes most sense for each conversation.

- What exactly does this position entail?
- Will I be required to clean restrooms?
- Will I be required to learn a computer system?
- What are the start and end dates of this position?
- How far in advance can we occupy the site?
- How much time after our last day worked can we occupy the site?
- Do you offer a completion bonus?
- How much is the completion bonus, or how is it calculated?
- Is there a set schedule or rotating schedule?
- Can I request a set schedule?
- Can couples work the same shift?
- Can we have the same/opposite days off?
- Can couples work opposite shifts?
- Can we have same/opposite days off?
- What type of training is provided?
- What is the dress code? Are uniforms provided?

- Are all hours paid? What is the pay rate?
- Is there a fee for the RV site?
- Is electric metered?
- How many hours are required for the site?
- Are extra hours provided at pay? How many?
- Is overtime available? Mandatory? How much?
- Does my schedule include weekend/nights/early mornings/holidays?
- What additional benefits are provided?
- What on-site amenities will I (my family) have access to?
- How many other working RVers do you have each season?
- How many returning RVers do you get each season?
- Do staff sites have full hookups?
- Is there a staff supplied honeywagon service? How often is it?
- Are staff RV sites separate from daily guests?
- How many monthly guests would you say you have?
- How is cell service in your area? Best carriers?
- How far is shopping? Groceries? Hospital? Gas? Walmart?
- Do you allow onsite RV washing and/or repairs?
- What is the percentage of guests for daily and seasonal sites?
- Do you have any past RV workers I can follow-up with?

SITES FOR JOB LISTINGS

You can find FREE job postings all over the web, so make sure you don't get caught paying for a sneak peek!

Thankfully, you won't have to invest a dime to see ALL the job ads for the sites I've listed in this chapter. These companies focus on helping the RV community find the information they need to get started, keep going and go farther! That's why we've highlighted them here for your reference!

ESCAPEES

https://rverjobexchange.com

You probably already know that Escapees RV Club is one of the longest-running, largest and quite possibly the most loved RV club and membership organization out there. Their mission is to provide a total support network for all RVers, which I think is pretty special and quite amazing!

As part of this total support network, Escapees created the RVer Job Exchange to help connect RVers to those companies that have RV jobs available! From workamping jobs to remote careers, there is a variety of job listings to choose from. Currently it includes free ads, a free resume builder and a resume listing service, where employers can easily search.

WORKAMPING JOBS

http://www.workampingjobs.com

If you're an RVer who's looking for seasonal, part-time of full-time campground jobs- this site is the place for you!

Completely FREE for both employers and RVers to use, this site is the perfect resource for workamping jobs.

Employers can submit listings for volunteer work, workamping jobs, paid positions or a combination. RV workers can also submit a detailed online resume to let employers know they are available and what they are looking for.

COOLWORKS

https://www.coolworks.com

Since 1995, CoolWorks has been one of the leaders in connecting people to seasonal jobs in awesome locations. They believe that you should love your job, and they are on a mission to make that happen!

On this site you'll find FREE job opportunities for everywhere from national parks to ski resorts to retreat centers, and everything in between. They also host an online journal which profiles the exciting stories from CoolWorkers who've been there and done that, along with a blog, shop and FREE members area with more personal interaction.

So whether you're still researching, need a seasonal job, or just feel the call to go explore, CoolWorks has got you covered.

WORKERS ON WHEELS

https://www.work-for-rvers-and-campers.com

Created by a husband and wife, who full-time travel and work along the way, Workers on Wheels is a mix of job listings and information. They host a mix of blogs and detailed listings about ways to earn on the go, as well as the actual job post listings, featured employers and a newsletter.

PEAKSEASON

https://www.peakseason.com

PeakSeason is a relatively new resource offering access to seasonal jobs. They do not focus primarily on RV jobs, although they do have a few, but offer many short-term solutions to those willing to put a bit more work into lining up camping in nearby areas.

The website is easy and FREE to search and offers an online account for job seekers. In your account you'll not only be able to setup job alerts to notify you of new job postings you might find interesting, but you'll also be able to create an online profile with social media links, add multiple resumes for different job types and create cover letters to send as well.

MORE FREE JOB SITES

Happy Vagabonds

https://www.happyvagabonds.com

Cradle of Forestry

https://cfaia.catsone.com/careers/

Recreation Resource Management

http://www.camphost.org

RV Park Store

https://www.rvparkstore.com/rv-park-help-wanted

American Land & Leisure

http://www.americanll.com

You can also check out larger job board sites and search for keywords like 'campground' and 'park host'

https://www.usajobs.gov

https://www.indeed.com

https://www.volunteer.gov

SAMPLE WORK AGREEMENT

September 9, 2018

Mrs. Employer
Company Name
1234 First Street
Anytown, State ZIP

Dear Mr & Mrs Workamper

We are excited you have agreed to join our team for the upcoming season! As a measure of good faith we ask that you read the following work agreement and provide a signed copy for our files.

Your position will start on March 3, 2019 and end   September 9, 2019. You are welcome to arrive up to five days in advance and stay an additional 5 days after your position ends.

Your site will be provided for FREE and will not be included in your wages on your W-2 statement, since we require you to stay onsite. The space we have reserved is site #512 and includes water, sewer, electric, cable and Wi-Fi.

You have agreed to work in our front office, as a Reservation Agent booking reservations for our guests and answering customer phone calls. Your schedule will rotate weekly, but you will work between 30-40 hours each week at a rate of 11.50 per hour.

We also pay a completion bonus at the end of the season, which is calculated at $1 for every hour worked.

Please sign and return a copy of this letter by fax or mail no later than September 15, 2018 .

We agree to the terms outline above:

_____   _____
Mrs. Employer Signature   Date   Mrs. Workamper Signature   Date

RV GLOSSARY

ARVC: National Association of RV Parks & Campgrounds

BLM: Bureau of Land Management

Black Water: Sewage

Blue Boy: A portable waste tank, usually blue in color.

Boondocking: Camping without utilizes.

Bunkhouse: RV models with bunkbeds.

Class A: Motorhome usually ranging from 26-40 feet in length.

Class B: Smaller van-like motorhomes.

Class C: Motorhome with cab section over driving area for sleeping or sometimes entertainment and storage.

Corps/USACE: US Army Corps of Engineers

Dry Camping: Boondocking- Camping without utilizes.

DOE: Depending On Experience

DW: Dry weight- the weight of the RV without supplies or passengers.

EOE: Equal Opportunity Employer

Extended Stay: Sites reserved for RVers who wish to stay for longer periods of time. Usually monthly or season.

FHU: Full hookups (water, electric, sewer)

Fifth Wheel: Pull behind RV type with special hitch inside the bed of a pickup truck.

FMCA: Family Motor Coach Association

Fresh Water: Water that is safe to drink.

Full-time: Traveling in an RV year-round.

Full-timer: Someone who lives in their RV full time

Galley: RV Kitchen

Grey Water: Used water from the kitchen, bathroom sinks and shower.

Hitch: Joint that is used to secure two vehicles for towing capability.

Hookups: Utilities like electric, water, sewer, and cable.

KOA: Kampgrounds of America- franchise of over 400 RV Parks

Locals: Refers to the local community. Non-RVers

NPS: National Park Service

Rig: Another term to describe your RV setup.

RV: Travel trailer, motorhome or 5th-wheel

RVIA: Recreation Vehicle Industry Association

Shore Power: Electricity provided by an external source.

Snowbirds: RVers who go South each winter

Sticks and Bricks: Traditional housing options.

Stipend: Fixed amount of money for expenses (i.e. food, fuel, etc.) paid to volunteers at government agencies or non-profits

Toad: Tow vehicle

Toy Hauler: RV with built in cargo space

Travel Trailer: Non-motorized RV units that need to be towed by a truck or large SUV.

TT: Thousand Trails Membership Club

USFS: U.S. Forest Service

USFWS: U.S. Fish & Wildlife Service

Volunteer: An individual who performs hours of service for a public agency or non-profit organization for civic, charitable, or humanitarian reasons

W/E/S: Water/Electric/Sewer

Wi-Fi: Wireless Internet Access

Winterize: Special steps to prepare the RV for Winter use and/or storage.

Working RVer: Someone who works part-time, full-time or seasonally while living in an RV

EPILOGUE

When I look back on our decision to travel full-time and live in an RV, sometimes it still surprises me that we actually did it! I mean there are many things we've wanted to do in life, including living on a sailboat, that we just haven't had the nerve to actually follow through with.

Fortunately, RV life was not one of them!

Living life on the road was a radical change for us and even more so for our family and friends, none of who live lives similar to ours. We didn't let negative comments or fear of the unknown stand in our way, and I firmly believe you should not either!

Over the past 5 years, we've had the privilege to visit over 30 states with our children and actually explore like locals, rather than tourists. We've met great people, seen some amazing new places, and done some pretty incredible things together as a family. These memories will stay with us for years to come and in all honesty, I have to admit this is by far the best part of going full-time.

We've met many people along our journey who praise the decision to go RVing at a younger age than traditionally acceptable. We were in our 20's when we started and although we didn't have the biggest or prettiest RV available (we actually had the opposite) we didn't care! We wanted to travel and try something new, so we made it happen! I'm always honest about this, and I'll say it again- it wasn't a walk in the park to learn how to RV, then adjust to living in one, and then figure out how to make money to keep the adventures going, but I wouldn't choose any other way!

So whatever age you are, if you are considering RV lifestyle and have a dream of traveling, I'd like to leave you with one piece of advice…

"Go Small & Go Now!"

Take a chance on adventure! Find a way that's comfortable and find a way to maintain it. Then set a date and just do it. Conquer your fears, prove your naysayers wrong and achieve this goal you set for yourself by any means necessary!

As always,

Safe Travels & Many Adventures

-Sharee

ABOUT THE AUTHOR

5 years ago, my husband Antwon & I decided to try something crazy and way outside of our comfort zone. We decided to buy an RV and live it in with our 4 kids.

Since that moment, life has taken us on some pretty epic adventures, and I went from not knowing what workamping was to writing articles about it while we experienced the lifestyle firsthand.

Those early days ultimately led to me now working behind the scenes as the Founder and Director of Operations for Live Camp Work, where I help connect both sides of the workamping community and encourage growth and new opportunities from within.

And in case you're wondering… "Yes! I'm still workamping!"

But, I'm also a travel blogger and entrepreneur.

I love to create products and services to help others be successful and save time and money! I've created several courses, both small and large, for RVers who need additional help, guidance or just an all-inclusive resource to help them get started. I'm also hoping to finish my 2nd book by the end of 2020- so stay tuned.

This book was 5 years in the making and I am so very thankful I finally found the courage to put it together. I sincerely thank you for reading along and having the curiosity to explore the unfamiliar!

I wish you the best-

Stay in touch on Facebook @LiveCampWork